JAGUAR XK-E

A SOURCE BOOK

EDITED AND ANNOTATED BY

Dale Sass

Motorbooks International
Publishers & Wholesalers Inc
Osceola, Wisconsin 54020, USA

Bookman Publishing/Baltimore, Maryland

Contents

This is the new Jaguar XK-E!

Forward

(This forward, written by Thomas E. Bonsall, first appeared as an article in the Spring 1984 issue of "Car Design" magazine. It is reprinted with their permission.)

Jaguar. The name itself conjures up exciting images of style and speed. For over half-a-century it has been so and this year, with the introduction of the first Jaguar soft-top in several seasons, the first new Jaguar six-cylinder engine in three decades and the first new Jaguar sedan in fifteen years waiting in the wings, it seems appropriate to look back on the history of this remarkable car and try to understand the reasons for its extraordinary appeal.

Probably more than any other important international marque, the Jaguar's impact has been due to its styling. The original SS model was little more than a superb styling exercise: the chassis was really rather ordinary and purchased on the "outside" from Standard Motor Company. Even in the postwar era, when Jaguar mechanicals were not only Jaguar designed and built but highly interesting technically, a seemingly endless trail of reliability problems often kept the full promise from being realized and it was still the fabulous Jaguar styling that brought the buyers in.

The Jaguar story began improbably enough with motorcycle sidecars. In 1921, William Lyons moved in with his family in their new residence in Blackpool, in the North of England. Lyons was a motorcycle enthusiast and was quite familiar with sidecars. Still, he had never seen anything like the sidecar owned by his new neighbor across the avenue, William Walmsley. By the standards of the day, Walmsley's "Swallow" sidecar was incredibly streamlined and racy. Lyons' shock was all the greater when he learned that Walmsley was actually manufacturing them himself in a little shop behind his parents' house. After a few months, a friendship blossomed between the young men and, in 1922, the Swallow Sidecar Company was officially formed by the two. They were notably successful in this early endeavor for much the same reason the Jaguar cars to come were successful: their styling. Swallow sidecars quickly became linked with the finest motorcycles of the period, especially the Brough, known as "the Rolls-Royce of motorcycles."* That was fine as far as it went, but Lyons, at least, wanted ultimately to expand into automobile manufacture. His chance came in 1926 with the hiring of Cyril Holland.

Holland was a trained automotive coachmaker and the first person hired by the firm solely for automotive purposes. He was to stay on until after the war and had enormous influence on early SS and Jaguar cars. His first automobile body, and the firm's very first as well, was done in 1926 as a dry run on a wrecked Talbot chassis. Early in 1927, one of Swallow's agents managed to smuggle a new Austin Seven chassis to Lyons and, from it and a design sketch, Cyril Holland built an Austin-Swallow, the prototype of the celebrated series of Swallow cars. By the middle of 1927, Austin was supplying a small number of chassis to Jaguar (through the front door, this time). The natty little cars caught on and a seemingly endless series of Hyphenated-Swallows

followed: Morris-Swallows, Clyno-Swallows, Fiat-Swallows, Wolseley-Swallows, Swift-Swallows and Standard-Swallows, among others. Soon the small factory in Blackpool was rendered hopelessly inadequate by mounting demand (to the delight of Lyons and the consternation of Walmsley) and, by 1928, the Swallow company had moved lock, stock and sidecars to a larger facility in Coventry in England's industrial Midlands.

The move was a fateful one for it put Swallow in close proximity to Standard and to Standard's general manager, John Black. Black saw considerable promise in the Swallow coachbuilding enterprise and soon agreed to develop a Standard 2-litre chassis especially for the car Lyons wanted to build: a low, racy grand touring coupe, the SS1. The first prototype was nearing completion when Lyons fell ill with appendicitis. In his absence, Walmsley had the roof raised to accommodate more passenger room. When Lyons got out of the hospital and saw the result, he was furious—but it was too late. Production had been promised for the 1931 motor show and there was no time to redo it. To Lyons' surprise (and relief), the cars went over quite well, even though both body and chassis proved extremely troublesome in customer hands. Over 700 were built. Lyons went back to the drawing board, lengthened and lowered the car, developed a new, under-slung frame and, in time for the 1932 show, the "real" SS1 was finally built. The SS was now regarded as a separate marque, the company had been renamed "SS Cars, Ltd." and, by 1935, a whole range of snazzy tourers was being built on an increasingly improved Standard chassis. Things were really moving quickly—too quickly for the less ambitious Walmsley, so he took his fortune and retired, leaving Lyons indisputably in charge.

That the SS models of this period were exciting to look at and offered remarkable value for the money, there was no doubt. They were not, however, true sports cars and lacked truly exciting performance. For 1935, however, a genuine sports car, the handsome "90," was built on a 2.5-litre chassis.

The first SS four-door sedan appeared in the latter months of 1935. It bore the "Jaguar" name and was the first SS model to do so. It was, in the SS tradition, very handsome and sporty and an exceptional value for the money. The first all-steel bodies were built in 1938, an effort that almost broke the company, but all was sorted out and the factory was finally humming along just in time for the outbreak of war in 1939. Some 5,000 cars were built in 1939, never-the-less.

The war brought unusual challenges to Jaguar, as might have been expected, and part of the solution was to return to large scale production of motorcycle sidecars for the army! The postwar era, however, would necessitate new and radical efforts to meet the changing marketplace. As first steps, the sidecar business was sold off and the name on the building was changed to, "Jaguar Cars, Ltd."

The first postwar cars were continuations, with refinements, of the successful prewar saloon models. Although the four-cylinder engines were still manufactured by Standard, the postwar sixes were designed and built by Jaguar. The first new postwar car, the 1949 Mark V sedan, was considered an interim model. It bore a striking resemblance to the "R" series Bentleys of the period and was a good illustration of the Jaguar philosophy in that it offered better performance and styling than the Bentley—and at a considerably lower price. (It also

---

* Rolls-Royce, evidently amused by all the instances of such comparative use of their name, once ran a magazine ad headlined, "And now, the Rolls-Royce of cars"!

revealed Jaguar's contempt for intelligible model designations! There had never been any Marks I through IV. After the Mark V, the Mark VI was nowhere to be seen as the company jumped directly to the Marks VII through X. While they were in production, the compact 2.4-litre sedan was built and superceded by an improved version known as the Mark II—whereupon the 2.4-litre became known retroactively as the Mark I. Got it?)

It was clear by this point that Jaguar's future lay in the export market. British government policies were mandating an export-or-die approach and Jaguar designed the Mark VII with export sales, particularly to the United States, in mind. Announced in 1950, the Mark VII was the most sophisticated Jaguar yet and had the massive, luxurious feel that Americans liked. Indeed, Lyons himself is on record as believing that this model was a tad too heavy in appearance (a self-criticism he also directed at the design of the later Mark X), but this opinion is not universally shared by enthusiasts. The Mark VII and its derivatives, the Marks VIII and IX, were the most popular Jaguars up to that time and are eagerly collected today. Over 30,000 of the Mark VIIs alone were manufactured between 1950 and 1957. In terms of their practical impact on the company, the Mark VII and the current XJ series were the two most important Jaguars ever built. Lyons was knighted in 1956 for his services to exports and the Mark VII was largely the car that did it.

Oddly enough, the Mark VII has been over-shadowed by a car originally intended as little more than a gimmick to draw publicity to it. The Mark VII had been delayed by production headaches and Jaguar officials thought it would be nice to fit the new twin-overhead-cam six developed for the big sedan into an exciting sports car body suitable for display at the motor shows. The result was the fabulous XK120 of 1949. The intention was to build two hundred or so of the hand-crafted, aluminum-bodied cars and let it go at that. Public reaction was such, however, that steel panels were quickly tooled and 12,000 XK120s were ultimately sold before production ended in 1954! And why not? Here was the proven Jaguar concept at work again. The XK120 was incredibly fast for its time (the "120" stood for the 120 mph top speed), it was startlingly good-looking and, compared to anything else with that sort of appeal, cheap. XK140 and XK150 versions were subsequently built up through 1960. In addition to its wide-ranging influence on other auto designers and manufacturers, the XK series finally convinced Jaguar officials that there was real money in sports cars. This led directly to Jaguar's successful racing programs of the Fifties which, in turn, led to the development of the great "C-," "D-" and "E-Type" sports cars by Lyons and Malcolm Sayer.

The D-Type was slated for production but a disastrous fire at the factory in 1957 wiped it out and the similar E-Type did not finally make its appearance until 1961. In its styling, the E-Type was one of the most spectacular sports cars of all time and is still a head-turner after all these years. It was extremely fast, too, whether in the original 3.4-litre form, or subsequent 4.2-litre and 5.3-litre V-12 versions. Its handling was a subject of controversy. Niggling details such as passenger compartment heating and ventilation were not accorded much attention at the factory, either. Still, its demise in 1975 was—and remains—a source of distress not only to Jaguar enthusiasts but also to lovers of exciting cars everywhere.

Throughout this period, however, it was the somewhat less exciting sedans that continued to produce most of the revenue and the most important of these prior to the XJ6 was the 2.4-litre "Mark I" of 1955. This car was what many Jaguar enthusiasts considered the traditional Jaguar, the classic sport sedan, something the Marks VII through X (and even the XJ) were simply too large to be. Performance was a bit anaemic at first with the 2.4, but a 3.4-litre engine was offered in 1957 and a 3.8 finally found

its way into the Mark II. In its styling, the Mark I was very much a little Mark VII, but more streamlined and modern. Lyons himself was disappointed by the "crab track" of the Mark I, but this was changed on the restyled Mark II and it is the subsequent versions that appeal most to collectors today.

The "S-Type" was announced in 1963. It was a modified Mark II, the main visual change being the lengthening of the tail, and it, too, was a popular car with buyers and collectors alike. After the acquisition of Daimler in 1960, Daimler versions of the Mark II (the Daimler V-8) and the S-Type (the Daimler Sovereign) were successfully marketed. Only the Daimler V-8 had a Daimler engine, however. The Sovereign and all subsequent Daimler sedans have been badge-engineered Jaguars. The last S-Type was manufactured in 1969.

The successor to the Mark VII-IX was the Mark X announced in 1961. The Mark X was not only the largest Jaguar ever built, it looked it. If anything, it looked even bigger than it actually was. Few enthusiasts, even among Jaguar specialists, have any particular love for the Mark X today and, even in retrospect, it seems singularly lacking in visual grace. It is a shame, too, because the Mark X was a splendid machine that could boast of much better performance than its dumpy looks suggested and a level of technical sophistication not previously reached on Jaguar vehicles. It continued in production until 1970 when XJ6 output was at last beginning to meet demand. In fact, the Mark X (or the 420G, as it was known in its later years) is still around in the form of the very British-looking Daimler limousine, an enormous vehicle fashioned largely from Mark X internal parts.

The XJ6, announced in 1968, was the last Jaguar over which Lyons had control. Fifteen years later, many enthusiasts still regard it as the most beautiful sedan in the world. It is also, indisputably, one of the most important Jaguar models in history—and the most popular by far. It has, almost alone, carried the Jaguar name across a decade-and-a-half of unparalleled change in the international automobile industry. It was originally powered by the famous Jaguar XK six, but a new V-12, designated the XJ12, appeared as a high performance alternative in 1971. (The Daimler equivalents were the Sovereign and the Double-Six). A spiritual successor to the luxury sedan Marks VII-X, more than to the sportier Mark I and its derivatives, the XJ series has a high degree of performance, none-the-less. A long-awaited successor, known as the AJ40, is slated for production a few months from now (as this is written).

With the passing of the E-Type, enthusiasts were hoping for a similar replacement. What they got was the sedan-based XJ-S, a highly civilized grand touring coupe more in the tradition of the original SS1 than that of the XKs. The general disappointment was heightened by the styling. The British and Americans both thought it looked too American. It also arrived in a recession and fuel-crisis rocked market that was not congenial to new arrivals. The result was a car that has never seemed to live up to its potential, despite many interesting features.

With the dawning of the Eighties, the fortunes of Jaguar Cars, Ltd., had fallen to a low ebb. The new chairman, John Egan, arrived with orders to fix it or kill it—and promptly set about doing the former, much to the relief of Jaguar enthusiasts who had feared a fate like that of the lamented MG. In the past three years, Jaguar quality, manufacturing efficiency and sales have each increased several times over and the company is making solid profits once more.

A replacement for the E-Type is even rumored to be in the works for the latter part of the decade. Lovers of exciting cars everywhere cannot help but be a little excited themselves as they watch Jaguar's return to health and the wealth of interesting new models and engineering achievements that have been announced.

Preface

Ask the average American to name a specific Jaguar model and more than likely the response will be "XK-E." Like no other Jaguar before or since, the XK-E epitomizes Jaguar's reputation for British speed, luxury and grace. The E-Type's 1961 introduction coincided with America's mushrooming demand for performance cars. During its fourteen year production run, over 72,000 XK-E's were built, and the vast majority of them were destined for the American market.

After World War II, the British auto industry offered a plethora of relatively low-volume luxury marques in Jaguar's market. Names like Alvis, Lea Francis, Invicta, Riley, Lagonda, Humber and Armstrong Siddeley, among others, were competing in the same price class. It was at that time that Jaguar first realized the importance of the large American market. Successful sales in the U.S. could make Jaguar's engineering and production facilities more cost effective, thus giving them an edge over the competition.

It was the XK-120 of 1948 that got Jaguar started on American shores, and the subsequent production of the XK-E that firmly implanted Jaguar's American reputation. In retrospect, Jaguar's post-war policy appears brilliant. Most of the British luxury cars extant at the end of the war have long since fallen by the wayside while today's Jaguar appears stronger than ever as it prepares to leave the British Leyland conglomerate and fend for itself once more. In fact, Jaguar has been the best-selling British car on the American market for the past few seasons. Thus, it seems more than fitting for the Jaguar XK-E to be included in Bookman Publishing's Source Book Series.

The British auto industry doesn't apply the same significance to model year changes that the U.S. auto industry does. Grilles and taillights are not altered each year in Britain simply for the sake of yearly differentiation. A more common British practice is to update a car after a number of years and christen it a "Series II" or "Mark II" model. If demand remains strong, a "Series III" or "Mark III" may follow. Consequently, this Source Book is structured differently than most of those on

American cars. There are not separate chapters for each model year (i.e., 1961, 1962, etc.). Instead, there is a chapter for each of the four XK-E models: the 3.8 Liter (1961-1964), the 4.2 Liter (1965-1968), the Series II 4.2 Liter (1969-1971) and, finally, the Series III 5.3 Liter (1971-1975).

Admittedly, there is a blur between the 4.2 Liter model and the Series II 4.2 Liter. Some of the Series II modifications were incorporated on earlier cars as running changes. (Sometimes these cars are referred to as Series 1½ models.) Also, there were a handful of Series III cars built with the 4.2 liter six cylinder engine instead of the V-12. It seems no matter how the rules are drawn up there will be exceptions!

This is the thirtieth volume in the Source Book Series. The idea was to collect in one place—and at an affordable price—all the important manufacturer's sales literature on a particular collectible car along with commentary about both the car and the literature. Clearly, the idea has caught on. This book includes many of the Jaguar brochures that originally listed the XK-E. Most of those items not actually selected for reproduction have been mentioned in the text that accompanies each chapter. Much of the literature is quite rare and—taken together—would cost many times the price of this book, assuming it could be found.

Thanks are definitely in order to a few special people. This project could not have been possible without Paul Brounstein's comprehensive collection of Jaguar XK-E sales literature, from which all of the literature reproduced in this book has been taken. Also, I wish to thank Sam Shields and the staff of Bookman Publishing, Tom Bonsall and Ed Lehwald, who, with Source Books of their own under their belts, provided a helping hand and needed moral support. Finally, I would like to thank my parents, William and Alice Sass, who bought me subscriptions to the British automotive weekly, "The Autocar," as a kid when my friends were reading "Mad Magazine" and "Superman" comics.

Long Beach, California
June, 1984

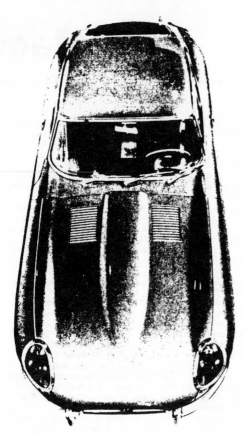

Champion, race-tested E-type 3.8 litre triple carburetor engine. Disc brakes and independent suspension on all four wheels.

New, integral body chassis based on Monocoque principle (light weight with extreme rigidity). Unique third door trunk compartment.

The Jaguar XK-E is the first truly new production sports car design in more than a decade. Develops 265 bhp at 5,500 rpm. One of the fastest production sports cars ever offered for public sale, the XK-E has a maximum speed of 150 mph.

Choice of two aerodynamic bodies: open two-seater with interchangeable hard or soft top, and all-steel coupe. See your local Jaguar dealer or write Jaguar Cars Inc., 32 East 57th Street, New York 22, N. Y.

3.8 Liter

In March, 1961, Jaguar unveiled the XK-E (or E-Type as it was known in Europe) at the Geneva Auto Show. It stole the show. Sir William Lyons, head of Jaguar Cars, Ltd., had done it again! It had been his policy to produce sedans and sports cars offering styling, luxury and performance on par with the finest marques of Europe at only half their cost. This new Jaguar was no exception. It combined Malcolm Sayer's contemporary ellipse styling with William Heynes' pedigreed engineering. In short, it looked and performed like an Italian GT car (Ferrari or Maserati) costing twice as much.

The XK-E was a culmination of many years of success in the field dating back to 1948. Many of its features appeared on earlier production and prototype models. The twin overhead camshaft six cylinder engine with seven main bearings was essentially the same design as that offered on the original XK-120 of 1948. Improvements were made continually over the years. A 3.8 Liter "S" variant with three SU carburetors and a redesigned head was introduced late in 1959 for the XK-150. This engine was used on the initial E-Types. Rack and pinion steering debuted on the XK-140 of 1954. Girling disc brakes came along later with the XK-150. Both of these features were incorporated into the XK-E. But, it was the competition D-Type and XK-SS (D-Type with road equipment) that foreshadowed the XK-E's aerodynamic bodywork. The D-Type was Malcolm Sayer's brainchild. He used the simple ellipse shape to fashion one of the most functional racing cars of all time, the D-Type of 1954. The D-Type's unit body monocoque structure was also used on the XK-E. Many of the suspension details for the E-Type were worked out on the smaller prototype E1A of 1958. The E1A also employed the familiar ellipse shape of the D-Type. Jaguar fielded a new racing prototype in 1960 intended to replace the successful D-Type. It was designated the E2A and featured ellipse styling similar to the D-Type and E1A. By this time it was obvious that future Jaguar sports cars would abandon the traditional upright radiator grille styling of the XK-150. The E2A's most significant engineering feature was independent rear suspension. The company had experimented with this during World War II on military vehicles, but the E2A was Jaguar's first sports car application of the feature. In addition to the E2A a Mark II sedan was built with independent rear suspension for testing purposes as well. When the XK-E arrived in 1961 its main design elements were well established.

It is difficult to remember now, but try to imagine Jaguar's competition in the spring of 1961. There was no Corvette Sting Ray or Studebaker Avanti, no Porsche 911 and certainly no Datsun 240-Z. Mercedes-Benz was still building the 190SL and, at twice the price, the 300SL, and both were getting a little dated. Other popular British six cylinder sports cars were the Austin Healey 3000 and the Triumph TR-3 (both almost decade-old designs). Only the Italians could match the styling and the performance of the XK-E, and they wanted twice as much money to do it. It was no wonder Jaguar, the first new sports car of the sixties, stole the show at Geneva.

Many Americans may remember the popular song from 1963, "Dead Man's Curve." It begins, "I was cruising in my Sting Ray late one night, when an XK-E pulled up on the right." You probably remember the rest. If not, it's not important. The point is the significance of the early XK-Es on the American market. Here was a British car getting equal billing with what was probably young America's most desired car.

Exports to the United States were very important to Jaguar. After World War II, it became obvious to Jaguar management that the British market alone could no longer support a competitive luxury car manufacturer. More cars needed to be sold to justify the staggering costs of research, development and manufacture. Exporting was the answer and the United States was the largest single market. Jaguar, more than any other British luxury car builder, realized this. During the fifties, up to 80% of sports car production was headed for North America. A similar percentage of XK-Es was earmarked for the U.S. This explains why Jaguar would call the car "XK-E" in North America and the "E-Type" in Europe. The XK sports cars of the fifties had been tremendously successful in the U.S. and the importance of the American market could certainly justify a separate name for the car.

While we're on the subject of names, the European E-Type name was not without its own peculiarities. There had been no "A-Type" or "B-Type." The "C-Type" was derived from "competition." It was the competition version of the XK-120. The "D-Type" was a road-racing car for LeMans style races. The factory built 67 of these cars from 1954 to 1957 when a fire halted production. Sixteen of these cars were converted to XK-SS models for use on public roads as personal transportation.

The XK-E sported some new features of its own. Independent rear suspension, as has been noted, was used for the first time on a production Jaguar. Power brakes were also used for the first time on any Jaguar. Dunlop built them under license from the American manufacturer, Kelsey-Hayes. The coupe featured a rear door that was hinged on the side (instead of at the top like a contemporary hatchback). The hood and front fenders were constructed in one piece. This single unit was hinged at the front, and when tilted up provided almost unlimited access to the engine compartment. A fiberglass hardtop was available for the roadster after May, 1962. Dunlop SP41 radial tires were on the options list in May, 1963. Although the XK-E was new in many respects it still retained much of its British character. The radiator style grille was gone but the wire wheels, leather upholstery and wood steering wheel remained.

Jaguar's official factory sponsored racing program ended with the D-Type. However, the factory helped distributors and drivers covertly by providing race prepared cars to their order. Twelve lightweight competition E-Types were built between March, 1963 and January, 1964. They were built for specific race car drivers. They were all roadsters with weight-saving aluminum alloy bodies. Removable alloy tops were included and used in place when the cars were raced. Even an aluminum cylinder block was cast for the engine. Fuel injection and ZF 5-speed transmissions were also used. Because only twelve of these cars were built, they are highly prized by collectors today. Car #7, originally built for Briggs Cunningham, was recently offered for sale in "Hemmings Motor News" for $119,000. In addition to these twelve cars, Jaguar subsequently built a pair of steel bodied cars with aluminum hoods and the competition drivetrain. The first one was a roadster. The second one was a coupe. Peter Lindner, a German Jaguar distributor, was one of the most active E-Type competitors. His car, #5 of the twelve lightweight models, was rebodied for 1964 competition by Malcolm Sayer. The top was fixed and the rear end was reformed into a more aerodynamic shape. Flush mounted spot lights were placed between the grille opening and the headlights. Later in the year, Lindner died in a racing accident at Monthery, France. Jaguar's covertly sponsored racing program came to an end after this. In addition to the fourteen competition cars previously mentioned there was one other factory prepared competition model of interest. Actually it was built in 1963 before any of the above mentioned fourteen cars. It was built for Dick Protheroe who had been the most successful driver in early E-Type competition. He finished second at Reims in June, 1963. In appreciation of his efforts Malcolm Sayer fashioned a low-drag fixed-top coupe for competition.

The original 3.8 Liter XK-E was sold from the spring of 1961 to the fall of 1964. Total production was 15,496. This was broken down pretty evenly between the open and the closed cars. Roadsters numbered 7,827 versus 7,669 coupes. The coupe was favored in the U.K. while roadsters were the more popular in the U.S. During the course of this three and a half year period only one appearance change was made. Early models featured external hood latches on the front fenders. Later models had an interior hood release that eliminated the external latches.

The original black E-Type catalogue, issued in at least three editions, is reproduced on pages 11-17. There was a white full-line Jaguar catalogue and similar folder issued in the U.S. that included the new model (see pages 18-29). Another American piece, a large full-line catalogue, with a close-up of a Mark X radiator on the cover, included the XK-E (see pages 30-36). There was also a similar small white folder on just the XK-E.

Background of Fame

No more famous background can be found anywhere than that which lies behind the Jaguar 'E' Type G.T. (Grand Touring) Models. Developed from the famous 'C' Type and 'D' Type Sports Racing Cars with their illustrious records of successes on the racetracks of the World, the 'E' Type G.T. Models are presented as elegant and luxuriously appointed road vehicles having an outstanding road performance and incorporating very many features derived from the vast store of experience gained in international competitive events.

Thus, the monococque form of construction incorporating a steel, stressed shell body with sub-frames for engine and rear components, stems directly from the famous 'C' and 'D' Types, whilst an entirely new development is the unique system of independent rear suspension which is the result of many years of research and trial.

The power unit is the world-famous XK 'S' Type 3·8 litre twin overhead camshafts engine, with three carburetters, which produces 265 horsepower and affords a road performance in which ultra rapid acceleration and high maximum speeds are matched by superlative braking power and the highest degree of controlability. Together, these attributes invest the 'E' Type G.T. with an extraordinarily high factor of safety.

A study of the complete specification contained in this catalogue will reveal that, in every particular, from basic principles to minute details, the Jaguar 'E' Type G.T. is, in truth, the most advanced sports car in the world.

THE JAGUAR "E" TYPE

G.T. FIXED HEAD COUPÉ

THE JAGUAR "E" TYPE

G.T. OPEN TWO-SEATER

THE JAGUAR "E" TYPE

Shown with fibreglass detachable hard t

G.T. OPEN TWO = SEATER

op which is offered as an optional extra.

JAGUAR XK-E ROADSTER

By victory after victory on the racetracks of the world, Jaguar has earned for itself a position in the very front rank of modern sports cars.

Five times winners at Le Mans, three times victors at Rheims, several times winners of the R. A. C. Tourist Trophy and victorious in innumerable other International and National events, the racetrack breeding of Jaguar is evident from the moment the wheel is handled.

All the accumulated wealth of knowledge and experience gained in the hard school of motor racing have been built into the new XK-E Jaguar models, one of the fastest production sports cars ever offered for public sale.

XK-E models are equipped with 3.8 litre twin overhead camshaft XK engines, with three carburetors, developing 265 b. h. p. at 5,500 r. p. m.'s, with straight port cylinder heads of high tensile aluminum alloy and with hemispherical combustion chambers.

These engines provide a new high level of performance, yet, notwithstanding the high speed potential of the XK-E, the Jaguar characteristics of smoothness, silence, tractability and road adhesion are such that complete and effortless mastery is in the hands of the driver at all times and at all speeds.

The construction of the XK-E is unique, since it comprises a stressed shell, all-steel body of patented monocoque construction, which was developed and proven in the famous "D" Type Jaguar competition car in many of the world's most grueling races.

This form of construction has made it possible to reduce weight drastically, without compromising strength or rigidity. The XK-E is, therefore, approximately 600 pounds lighter than its predecessor, which makes this car capable of truly outstanding performance.

The two-door, two-seater bodies possess extremely low drag

characteristics, resulting from extensive wind-tunnel tests.

To compensate for the very high potential of which the **XK-E** models are capable, a suspension system has been designed to give brilliant roadholding characteristics under all driving conditons.

Independent front suspension incorporates transverse wishbones and torsion bars controlled by telescopic hydraulic dampers. Anti-roll bars are fitted to lower wishbones. Fully independent rear suspension incorporates, on each side, a lower transverse tubular link pivoted at the wheel carrier and subframe adjacent to the differential case and, above this, a halfshaft jointed at each end.

Longitudinal location is provided by the rubber mountings locating the assembly in the body structure and by a radius arm between the lower link and a mounting point on the body structure. Twin coil springs, each enclosing a telescopic hydraulic damper, provide the suspension medium. The whole assembly, together with the differential unit, is carried in an easily detachable subframe which is located in the body structure by rubber mountings.

An entirely new braking system has been developed for the **XK-E** models. It comprises Dunlop bridge-type four-wheel disc brakes, featuring quick-change pads. The front discs are fitted to the wheel hubs, while the rear discs are inboard, to reduce unsprung weight. The brake pedal operates twin master cylinders through a compensating device, which divides the system into two entirely independent hydraulic systems to the front and rear brakes.

Jaguar is proud to introduce the **XK-E Two-Seater Sports** Cars to that segment of the motoring public that places strong emphasis upon very high performance and safety; indeed, the highest performance ever offered at such modest cost.

Twin bucket seats, adjustable for
reach, upholstered in finest leather
over foam rubber; adjustable three-
spoke steering wheel of polished
lightweight alloy, with wood rim;
wind-up windows; console for radio
and twin speakers.

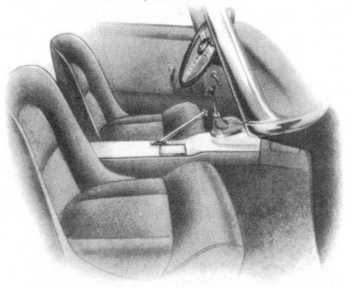

Interchangeable hard or soft convertible
top. Three section instrument panel,
with R.P.M. Counter, 160 m.p.h.
speedometer; oil pressure, water
temperature and fuel gauges; fuel
and brake fluid warning lights.

Row of labelled tumbler switches controlling auxiliary equipment; wide-angle, vertically adjustable mirror incorporating anti-dazzle secondary position; deep pile carpets over thick felt underlay.

Large counterbalanced door at rear, with release catch located in car, incorporates window and gives unobstructed access to luggage compartment, spare wheel and tools; hinged luggage container behind seats drops down to increase floor space if desired.

JAGUAR XK-E COUPE

SPECIFICATIONS — XK-E ROADSTER — BODY AND

APPOINTMENTS: Two-door two-seater body of extremely low drag characteristics resulting from intensive wind tunnel testing. The folding top, incorporating a large rear window, is of finest quality mohair, mounted on a special frame to permit single-handed erection or stowing. Fibreglass, detachable, hardtop available as an optional extra. Hardtop can be fitted without removing stowed top. Counterbalanced, forward-opening front section provides excellent accessibility to all mechanical components. Wrap-around windshield and thin pillars provide superb forward visibility. Door windows completely concealed within doors when fully lowered. Wrap-around bumpers with overriders at front and rear. Twin bucket seats, adjustable for reach, upholstered in finest quality Vaumol leather over Dunlopillo foam rubber cushions. Three-section instrument panel. Windshield rail and panel in mat-grained finish to eliminate reflection. Comprehensive instrumentation with 5-in. revolution counter, incorporating an electric clock, and 5-in. 160 m.p.h. speedometer, incorporating total and trip distance recorder, positioned in front of driver. Central panel contains separate instruments for electrically operated oil pressure, water temperature, fuel gauge with low-level warning light, and ammeter, together with a row of labelled tumbler switches controlling ancillary equipment. Separate housing beneath panel contains a radio and twin speakers (optional extra) together with an ashtray. When no radio is fitted, the speaker grilles are retained and the radio control panel aperture is blanked off with an escutcheon. Panel in front of passenger contains an open-fronted glove compartment and grab-handle. Three-spoked polished-alloy lightweight steering wheel with wood rim and central horn push. Wide-angle vertically-adjustable rear-view mirror incorporating anti-dazzle secondary mirror position. Deep pile carpets over thick felt underlay. Luggage accommodation provided in rear of car with access via a hinged-panel controlled from inside the car.

BODY CONSTRUCTION: Stressed shell all steel body of unique patented monocoque construction. Front subframe of square section steel tubing carries engine unit, suspension and forward hinged front section.

BRAKES: Dunlop bridge-type 4-wheel disc brakes, featuring quick change pads. Front brakes fitted on wheel hubs, rear brakes fitted inboard. Bellows-type brake servo—operating directly onto brake pedal. Pedal operates twin master cylinders through a compensator device which divides the system into two entirely independent hydraulic systems to front and rear brakes. Centrally positioned handbrake operates on rear wheels only. Brake fluid level warning light operates on both systems.

DIMENSIONS (Principal): Wheelbase, 8 ft. 0 ins.; track, front and rear, 4 ft. 2 ins.; over-all length, 14 ft. 7-5/16 ins.; over-all width, 5 ft. 5-1/4 ins.; over-all height, 4 ft. 0 ins.; ground clearance (laden), 5-1/2 in.; dry weight, 2,464 lbs. approx.

ELECTRICAL EQUIPMENT: Lucas 12-volt system. Large capacity battery giving 57 amp./hour at 10-hour rate with current voltage control. Ventilated dynamo. Eight fuse control box, fully labelled, located behind hinged-central instrument panel for ease of access. Side lamps. Lucas PL 700 headlamps with hand-operated dimmer-switch on instrument panel. Separate lever actuating headlamp flashing. Separate stop, tail, direction and reflector units mounted in a single assembly. Rear number plate lamps. Self-cancelling, flashing direction indicators and warning light on panel. Instruments and labelled switches illuminated by internal floodlighting controlled by a two-position dimmer switch. Map reading light. Interior light. Twin-blended note horns. Triple-blade, two-speed, self-parking, windshield wiper unit. Electrically operated windshield washers. Cigarette lighter with luminous socket. Starter motor.

Vacuum and centrifugal automatic ignition control. Oil coil ignition. Wiring harness in quickly detachable front body section connected to main circuits through an eight pin connector mounted on engine compartment bulkhead.

ENGINE: Six cylinder twin overhead camshaft 3.8-litre XK Jaguar "S" type engine. 87 mm. bore by 106 mm. stroke (3.425 ins. x 4.1732 ins.). Cubic capacity 3,781 c.c. (230.6 ins.). Compression ratio 9:1. Power output (9:1): 265 b.h.p. at 5,500 r.p.m.; torque: 260 ft. lbs. at 4,000 r.p.m. Three S.U. carburetors, type H.D.8 with manual choke control. Forced lubrication by submerged pump system incorporating a full flow filter. Chrome iron cylinder block fitted with dry type cylinder liners. Special "straight port" cylinder head of high tensile aluminum alloy featuring hemispherical combustion chambers and twin overhead camshafts operating large valves of 70° included angle. Aluminum alloy pistons. Steel connecting rods fitted with lead indium big end bearings. 2¾ ins. diameter counterweighted crankshaft carried on seven large lead indium bearings. Pressurized cooling system with thermostatically controlled electrically driven fan.

FUEL SUPPLY: 16¾ gallon tank capacity. Lucas electric pump. Gas filter incorporated into fuel line and located in engine compartment.

HEATING AND DEMISTING: High-output fresh air heating and multi-point windshield demisting system incorporating a two-speed fan controlled by switch on panel. Temperature and volume of air controls on panel. Ducts direct air to each side of compartment.

JACKING: Centrally located jacking posts enable the front and rear wheels on either side of the car to be raised simultaneously by means of the jack provided.

SPARE WHEEL AND TOOLS: The spare wheel is carried beneath the trunk floor in a separate compartment and is readily accessible. Fitted tool kit housed in the spare wheel compartment.

SUSPENSION: Independent front suspension incorporating transverse wishbones and torsion bars controlled by telescopic hydraulic dampers. Anti-roll bar fitted to lower wishbones. Fully independent rear suspension incorporating, on each side, a lower transverse tubular link pivoted at the wheel carrier and subframe adjacent to the differential case and, above this, a halfshaft universally jointed at each end. These serve to locate wheel in a transverse plane. Longitudinal location is provided by the rubber mountings locating the subassembly in the body structure and by a radius arm between the lower link and a mounting point on the body structure. Twin coil springs, each enclosing a telescopic hydraulic damper provide the suspension medium. The whole assembly together with the differential unit is carried in an easily detachable subframe which is located in the body structure by rubber mountings.

STEERING: Rack and Pinion. 16 in. steering wheel with separate adjustments for height and reach. 2¾ turns from lock to lock. Turning circle, 37 ft.

TRANSMISSION: Manually-operated four-speed, single helical synchromesh gearbox. Centrally positioned gear-shift lever. Synchromesh on top, third and second gear ratios. Borg & Beck 10 in. single dry-plate clutch with hydraulic operation. Hardy-Spicer Needle-Bearing propeller shaft. Hypoid rear axle fitted with limited-slip differential. Ratios 3.3:1. Optional axle ratios are available.

WHEELS AND TIRES: Wire-spoke wheels with center-lock hubs fitted with Dunlop 6.40 x 15 type RS.5 tires and tubes. Optional tire and wheel equipment available for racing: 6.00 x 15 front, 6.50 x 15 rear on special wheels.

SPECIFICATIONS—XK-E COUPE—BODY AND APPOINT-

MENTS: Two-door two-seater body of extremely low drag characteristics resulting from intensive wind tunnel testing. Counterbalanced forward opening front section provides excellent accessibility to all mechanical components. Large counterbalanced door at rear, with release catch located in car, incorporates rear window and gives unobstructed access to luggage compartment, spare wheel and tools. Lipped-shelf provided immediately behind seats for small parcels etc., and whole of body behind seats available for luggage. Hinged luggage-retainer at front of compartment drops down to increase floor space if required. Large window area together with wrap-around windshield and thin screen pillars provide superb all round visibility. Door windows completely concealed within doors when fully lowered. Hinged rear-quarter windows. Wrap-around bumpers with overriders at front and rear. Chrome finishers on rain gutter and windshield frame. Twin bucket seats, adjustable for reach, upholstered in finest quality Vaumol leather over Dunlopillo foam rubber cushions. Three section instrument panel together with windshield rail mat-grained finish to eliminate reflections. Comprehensive instrumentation with 5-in. revolution counter, incorporating an electric clock, and 5-in. 160 m.p.h. speedometer, incorporating total and trip distance recorder, positioned in front of driver. Central panel contains separate instruments for electrically operated oil pressure, water temperature, fuel gauge, with low-level warning light, and ammeter, together with a row of labelled tumbler switches controlling ancillary equipment. Separate housing beneath panel contains a radio and twin speakers (optional extra) together with an ashtray. When no radio is fitted, the speaker grilles are retained and the radio control panel aperture is blanked off with an escutcheon. Panel in front of passenger contains an open-fronted glove compartment and grab handle. Three-spoke polished alloy lightweight steering wheel with wood rim and central horn push. Sun visors for driver and passenger. Wide-angle vertically-adjustable rear-view mirror incorporating anti-dazzle secondary mirror position. Deep pile carpets over thick felt underlay.

BODY CONSTRUCTION: Stressed shell all steel body of unique patented monocoque construction. Front subframe of square section steel tubing carries engine unit, suspension and forward hinged front section.

BRAKES: Dunlop bridge-type 4-wheel disc brakes, featuring quick change pads. Front brakes fitted on wheel hubs, rear brakes fitted inboard. Bellows-type brake servo-operating directly onto brake pedal. Pedal operates twin master cylinders through a compensator device which divides the system into two entirely independent hydraulic systems to front and rear brakes. Centrally positioned handbrake operates on rear wheels only. Brake fluid level warning light operates on both systems.

DIMENSIONS (Principal): Wheelbase, 8 ft. 0 ins.; track, front and rear, 4 ft. 2 ins.; over-all length, 14 ft. 7-5/16 ins.; over-all width, 5 ft. 5-1/4 ins.; over-all height, 4 ft. 0 ins.; ground clearance (laden), 5-1/2 ins.; dry weight, 2,520 lbs. approx.

ELECTRICAL EQUIPMENT: Lucas 12-volt system. Large capacity battery giving 57 amp./hour at 10-hour rate with current voltage control. Ventilated dynamo. Eight fuse control box, fully labelled, located behind hinged-central instrument panel for ease of access. Side lamps. Lucas PL 700 headlamps with hand-operated dimmer-switch on instrument panel. Separate lever actuating headlamp flashing. Separate stop, tail, direction and reflector units mounted in a single assembly. Rear number plate lamps. Self-cancelling, flashing direction indicators and warning light on panel. Instruments and labelled switches illuminated by internal floodlighting controlled by a two-position dimmer switch. Map reading light. Interior light. Twin-blended note horns. Triple-blade, two-speed, self-parking, windshield wiper unit. Electrically operated windshield washers. Cigarette lighter with luminous socket. Starter motor. Vacuum and centrifugal automatic ignition control. Oil coil ignition. Wiring harness in quickly detachable front body section connected to main circuits through an eight pin connector mounted on engine compartment bulkhead.

ENGINE: Six cylinder twin overhead camshaft 3.8-litre XK Jaguar "S" type engine. 87 mm. bore by 106 mm. stroke (3.425 ins. x 4.1732 ins.). Cubic capacity 3,781 c.c. (230.6 ins.). Compression ratio 9:1. Power output (9:1): 265 b.h.p. at 5,500 r.p.m.; torque: 260 ft. lbs. at 4,000 r.p.m. Three S.U. carburetors, type H.D.8 with manual choke control. Forced lubrication by submerged pump system incorporating a full flow filter. Chrome iron cylinder block fitted with dry type cylinder liners. Special "straight port" cylinder head of high tensile aluminum alloy featuring hemispherical combustion chambers and twin overhead camshafts operating large valves of 70° included angle. Aluminum alloy pistons. Steel connecting rods fitted with lead indium big end bearings. 2¾ in. diameter counterweighted crankshaft carried on seven large lead indium bearings. Pressurized cooling system with thermostatically controlled electrically driven fan.

FUEL SUPPLY: 16¾ gallon tank capacity. Lucas electric pump. Gas filter incorporated into fuel line and located in engine compartment.

HEATING AND DEMISTING: High-output fresh air heating and multi-point windshield demisting system incorporating a two-speed fan controlled by switch on panel. Temperature and volume of air controls on panel. Ducts direct air to each side of compartment.

JACKING: Centrally located jacking posts enable the front and rear wheels on either side of the car to be raised simultaneously by means of the jack provided.

SPARE WHEEL AND TOOLS: The spare wheel is carried beneath the trunk floor in a separate compartment and is readily accessible. Fitted tool kit housed in the spare wheel compartment.

SUSPENSION: Independent front suspension incorporating transverse wishbones and torsion bars controlled by telescopic hydraulic dampers. Anti-roll bar fitted to lower wishbones. Fully independent rear suspension incorporating, on each side, a lower transverse tubular link pivoted at the wheel carrier and subframe adjacent to the differential case and, above this, a halfshaft universally jointed at each end. These serve to locate wheel in a transverse plane. Longitudinal location is provided by the rubber mountings locating the subassembly in the body structure and by a radius arm between the lower link and a mounting point on the body structure. Twin coil springs, each enclosing a telescopic hydraulic damper provide the suspension medium. The whole assembly together with the differential unit is carried in an easily detachable subframe which is located in the body structure by rubber mountings.

STEERING: Rack and Pinion. 16 in. steering wheel with separate adjustments for height and reach. 2¾ turns from lock to lock. Turning circle, 37 ft.

TRANSMISSION: Manually-operated four-speed, single helical synchromesh gearbox. Centrally positioned gear-shift lever. Synchromesh on top, third and second gear ratios. Borg & Beck 10 in. single dry-plate clutch with hydraulic operation. Hardy-Spicer Needle-Bearing propeller shaft. Hypoid rear axle fitted with limited-slip differential. Ratios 3.3:1. Optional axle ratios are available.

WHEELS AND TIRES: Wire-spoke wheels with center-lock hubs fitted with Dunlop 6.40 x 15 type RS.5 tires and tubes. Optional tire and wheel equipment available for racing: 6.00 x 15 front, 6.50 x 15 rear on special wheels.

XK-E COUPE

SEATING DIAGRAMS & GENERAL DIMENSIONS

SPECIFICATIONS

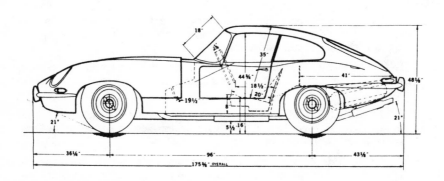

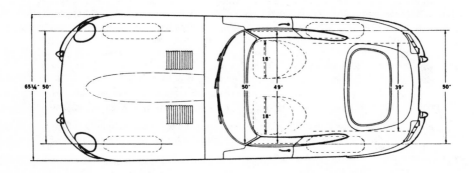

JAGUAR XK-E COUPE
JAGUAR XK-E ROADSTER

By victory after victory on the racetracks of the world, Jaguar has earned for itself a position in the very front rank of modern sports cars.

Five times winners at Le Mans, three times victors at Rheims, several times winners of the R. A. C. Tourist Trophy and victorious in innumerable other International and National events, the racetrack breeding of Jaguar is evident from the moment the wheel is handled.

All the accumulated wealth of knowledge and experience gained in the hard school of racing have been built into the new XK-E Jaguar models, one of the fastest production sports cars ever offered for public sale.

XK-E models are equipped with 3.8 litre twin overhead camshaft XK engines, with three carburetors, developing 265 b.h.p. at 5,500 r.p.m., with straight port cylinder heads of high tensile aluminum alloy and with hemispherical combustion chambers.

These engines provide a new high level of performance, yet, notwithstanding the high speed potential of XK-E, the Jaguar characteristics of smoothness, silence, tractability and road adhesion are such that complete and effortless mastery is in the hands of the driver at all times and at all speeds.

The construction of the XK-E is unique, since it comprises a stressed shell, all-steel body of patented monocoque construction, which was developed and proven in the famous "D" Type Jaguar competition car in many of the world's most grueling races.

This form of construction has made it possible to reduce weight drastically, without compromising strength or rigidity. The XK-E is, therefore, approximately 600 pounds lighter than its predecessor, which makes this car capable of truly outstanding performance.

The two-door, two-seater bodies possess extremely low drag characteristics, result-ing from extensive wind-tunnel tests.

To compensate for the very high potential of which the XK-E models are capable, a suspension system has been designed to give brilliant roadholding characteristics under all driving conditions.

Independent front suspension incorporates transverse wishbones and torsion bars controlled by telescopic hydraulic dampers. Anti-roll bars are fitted to lower wishbones. Fully independent rear suspension incorporates, on each side, a lower transverse tubular link pivoted at the wheel carrier and subframe adjacent to the differential case and, above this, a jointed halfshaft.

Longitudinal location is provided by the rubber mountings locating the assembly in the body structure and by a radius arm between the lower link and a mounting point on the body structure. Twin coil springs, each enclosing a telescopic hydraulic damper, provide the suspension medium. The whole assembly, together with the differential unit, is carried in an easily detachable subframe which is located in the body structure by rubber mountings.

An entirely new braking system has been developed for the XK-E models. It comprises Dunlop bridge-type four-wheel disc brakes, featuring quick-change pads. The front discs are fitted to the wheel hubs, while the rear discs are inboard, to reduce unsprung weight. The brake pedal operates twin master cylinders through a compensating device, which divides the system into two entirely independent hydraulic systems to the front and rear brakes.

Jaguar is proud to introduce the XK-E Two-Seater Sports Cars to that segment of the motoring public that places strong emphasis upon very high performance, luxury and safety; indeed the highest performance and prestige ever offered at such modest cost.

XK-E COUPE

Large counterbalanced door at rear, with release catch located in car, incorporates window and gives unobstructed access to luggage compartment, spare wheel and tools, hinged luggage container behind seats drops down to increase floor space if desired.

4.2 Liter

In October, 1964, Jaguar announced the 4.2 Liter version of the XK-E. This new model looked almost identical to the previous 3.8 Liter version. In fact, the only discernible difference on the exterior was the 4.2 badge mounted on the trunk. Beneath the unchanged body, however, were a number of modifications designed to correct the minor irritations of the earlier cars. The competition had announced new models. The Corvette Sting Ray was here. Plus, the Germans were fielding a new Mercedes 230SL and a new Porsche 911. This was no time to rest on earlier laurels.

There were a number of modifications to the 4.2 Liter model in 1964, all of which improved an already outstanding car. The obvious change to the new XK-E was the larger engine. It was initially bored out to provide increased pulling power for the large Mark X sedan. But the E-Type also benefited from the increased torque. New pistons and rings were used that reduced the excessive oil consumption that plagued earlier 3.8 Liter models. An electric fuel pump was new that year as well as an alternator. New seats with more padding and an adjustable rake improved interior comfort. Probably the most noticeable improvement for drivers was the new four-speed transmission with synchromesh in all gears. This was a vast improvement over the old unit and rectified the weakest link in the Jaguar drivetrain. Late in 1965, emergency flashers were made part of basic equipment. During 4.2 Liter production, air conditioning became available on left-hand drive units. Here, again, the importance of the American market is underscored. In conjunction with air conditioning came a new vertical flow radiator with twin electric fans. There had been complaints from warmer climates that the cooling system had been inadequate. With the addition of air conditioning, this new radiator was a virtual necessity. The new radiator eventually appeared on right-hand drive models, but the air conditioning was never offered to home-market customers.

In March, 1966, a third model was added to the XK-E range: the 2+2. This model did not replace the two-passenger coupe already in production, but supplemented it. The 2+2 was an attempt to add a grand touring car to the XK-E line. Although quarters were cramped, there was room for two more passengers in the rear. The 2+2 was a larger car than the two-passenger models. It stood two inches higher to provide headroom in the rear and it was stretched nine inches in length to accommodate the rear seat passengers. From the outside, most of the additional length was in the door. This allowed for access to the rear compartment. The weight penalty was about two hundred pounds for this increased size. Consequently, the 2+2 was slightly slower than its two-passenger counterpart.

In addition to the obviously increased passenger room, there was a side benefit to this new 2+2 model. The increased length provided room to install an automatic transmission. While this may sound like heresy to traditional sports car buffs, it must be kept in mind that 80% of XK-E production was destined for the United States. The vast majority of Americans preferred their cars with automatic transmissions. So there was a definite market for such a car. Even without the new automatic transmission, the 2+2 was the most costly of the E-Types. At about $5200 in the U.K. it listed for about $800 more than the roadster and almost $600 more than the two-passenger coupe.

In mid-1967, E-Types were no longer built with glass headlight covers. This was only the third exterior change in 6 1/2 years. The deletion of the external hood latches and the addition of the 4.2 badge were the two previous changes. Compared to them this was far more obvious and a portent of things to come as well. During the mid-sixties the U.S. government mandated safety requirements for all cars sold in the United States. The importance of the U.S. market to Jaguar made it necessary for Jaguar to comply. In the fall of 1968 the factory announced a Series II 4.2 Liter XK-E incorporating all of these Federal changes. But, prior to this, some running changes were made. The removal of the glass headlight cover was the first such change as well as the most obvious. During the spring of 1968 the redesigned dash was put into production. Dash switches were changed to a more flush rocker design for occupant safety. The ignition switch was moved to a safer position and the starter button was eliminated. A lid was put on the glove box as well.

Almost 23,000 4.2 Liter XK-Es were produced from the fall of 1964 to the fall of 1968 when the Series II models were announced. This was an annual average of about 5,700 cars per year, slightly less than the yearly average of 6,200 per year of the 3.8 Liter models. The production breakdown by body style included 9,545 roadsters, 7,770 two-passenger coupes and 5,598 2+2 coupes. Again, the closed cars were overwhelmingly popular in Britain. With the addition of the 2+2 model, closed cars outsold open cars in the U.S., as well. Although the first E-Type displayed at the Geneva show was a coupe, the car was originally designed as a roadster. Production figures clearly show the wisdom of adding the closed models.

British literature on the 4.2 Liter included a red folder in at least two editions (see pages 38-40), and a similar white folder dated 10/67 (see pages 42-43). The 2+2 was covered in a large white catalogue in editions undated and dated 8/67 and 7/68 (see pages 46-54). There was also a small black full-line Jaguar catalogue dated 10/67 covering the "1968" models (see pages 70-72). American literature included a folder on the XK-E coupe and roadster, and from which the cover art used on this book has been taken, (see pages 44-45). There were at least three similar sheets, two in color and one black-and-white. Folder and sheets were revised with the introduction of the 2+2 (see pages 55-57). The featured cover car was a yellow 2+2. There were also separate 2+2 folder and sheet items featuring a red 2+2. There was a small, white full-line black-and-white catalogue in the U.S. in 1967 (see pages 58-60) a small black-and-white folder in 1968 (see page 61) and similar full-line color brochures, a catalogue and a folder, issued in 1968-69 (see pages 62-69).

NEW 4·2 LITRE 'I

join the famous range of Mark Ten, 'S

E' TYPE MODELS

" model, Mark 2 and 'E' Type Jaguars

In response to a world wide demand, Jaguar proudly introduce into the present range a more powerful model which, whilst retaining the characteristics—aerodynamic body, disc brakes and independent suspension on all four wheels, which have made the 'E' type world famous, embodies many new technical advancements combining to give maximum performance with saloon car comfort.

A new 4.2 litre XK engine of advanced design steps up performance to an entirely new level and, together with the new all synchromesh gearbox, New effortless braking, New alternator, Pre-engaged starter, New "shaped" seating, still further improves that " special kind of motoring which no other car in the world can offer."

NEW ALTERNATOR gives greatly increased current supply over wide range of engine speeds, ensuring adequate current supply—even with city driving—for the extensive electrical service embodied.

PRE-ENGAGED STARTER facilitates starting under conditions of extreme cold.

SHAPED SEATING designed for maximum comfort, and upholstered in finest quality Vaumol leather over Dunlopillo foam rubber cushions.

JAGUAR

Grace...Space...Pace

BY APPOINTMENT
TO H.M. QUEEN ELIZABETH
THE QUEEN MOTHER
MOTOR CAR MANUFACTURERS
JAGUAR CARS LTD

The Jaguar 'E' type is a unique combination of graceful styling, luxurious interiors, smooth unobtrusive high performance, all of which are the hallmarks of this, the world's most outstanding G.T. car. The 4.2 litre 'XK' engine is fitted as standard to all 'E' type models and provides outstanding acceleration and flexibility of performance throughout its very wide speed range. Each model features rich upholstery, fitted carpets, extensive safety padding, comprehensive instrumentation and fresh air heating and ventilation. Each model combines outstanding handling with the luxury of saloon car comfort — a special kind of motoring which no other car in the world can offer.

ALTERNATOR gives greatly increased current supply over wide range of engine speeds, ensuring adequate current supply—even with city driving—for the extensive electrical service embodied.

PRE-ENGAGED STARTER facilitates starting under conditions of extreme cold.

SHAPED SEATING designed for maximum comfort, and upholstered in finest quality Vaumol leather over Dunlopillo foam rubber cushions.

JAGUAR
Grace...Space...Pace

Jaguar
4.2 XK-E
Coupe
& Roadster

"A different breed of cat"

OFTEN DESCRIBED as one of the world's most breathtaking sports cars and a "classic of the future," the new 4.2-liter Jaguar XK-E owes its basic design to a long racing heritage.

Available in two styles — roadster and coupe — its specifications are similar except in minor details. Its all-steel body is of Jaguar patented monocoque construction, a form that results in maximum strength, rigidity and lightness. Not only beautiful but functional, it was developed from extensive wind-tunnel testing and racing experience. Its four-wheel independent suspension is also competition-based and provides the driver with complete assurance at all times, along with outstanding comfort and freedom from road noises.

Powering the XK-E is the famed Jaguar XK engine that sped competition cars at the grueling 24 Hour race of LeMans to 5 wins in 7 years. Rugged and reliable, it moves the XK-E to 140 mph. and gives great performance character istics in the lower and mid-speed ranges. Coupled with this is a completely new crashproof all synchro-mesh, four-speed gearbox with a diaphragm clutch that gives smooth, progressive engagement with light pedal pressure.

Disc brakes at all four wheels are standard equipment — as are most of the features often considered "extras." But, praiseworthy as any description of the XK-E might be, the one true way to get to know the XK-E is to drive it. One brief spell behind the wheel will convince you that Jaguar is a "different breed of cat."

45

The graceful monocoque body, luxuriously furnished, provides ull headroom
room.   Wide, deep doors facilitate ease of access to front and rear seats
Dunlopillo cushions. A wide range of front seat adjustment, together
tallest of drivers to be accommodated in maximum comfort. Comprehensive
non-reflecting facia.   Full width shelf, a glove locker and a compartment beneath
air heating and ventilating system has individual direction controls for driver

ront and rear. Low floor design gives adequate leg and foot
which are upholstered in finest quality Vaumol leather over deep
with a steering wheel adjustable for reach and height, allows even the
instrumentation and clearly labelled control switches mounted in
centre arm rest provide ample space for personal effects.   Fresh
and passenger sides of car.

Specification

ENGINE. 6 cylinder, twin overhead camshaft, 4.2 litre XK Jaguar engine. 92.07 mm. bore, 106 mm. stroke (3.625″ by 4.1732″), cubic capacity 4235 c.c. (258.43 cu. ins.). Compression ratio 9 : 1 (8 : 1 optional). Power output (9 : 1) 265 b.h.p. at 5,400 r.p.m., torque 283 ft./lb. at 4,000 r.p.m. Three S.U. carburetters, Type HD.8 with manual choke control. Forced lubrication by submerged pump system incorporating a Full Flow Filter. Chrome iron cylinder block fitted with dry type cylinder liners. Special 'straight port' cylinder head of high tensile aluminium alloy featuring hemispherical combustion chambers and twin overhead camshafts operating large valves of 70° included angle. Aluminium alloy pistons. Steel connecting rods fitted with lead indium big end bearings. 2¾ ins. diameter counterweighted crankshaft carried on seven large lead indium bearings. Pressurised cooling system with thermostatically controlled, electrically driven fan.

TRANSMISSION. (Manually operated gearbox). Four speed, single helical all synchromesh gearbox. Ratios: Top, 3.07; 3rd, 4.07; 2nd, 6.06; 1st, 9.33; Reverse, 9.45. Centrally positioned change speed lever. Baulk ring synchromesh on all four forward ratios. Laycock Hausserman 10″ diaphragm clutch. Hardy-Spicer needle bearing propeller shaft. Hypoid rear axle. Ratio, 3.07 : 1. Differential unit mounted in sub-frame carrying the rear suspension.

TRANSMISSION. (Automatic Transmission model). Borg Warner Model 8 with dual drive range D1/D2. Gear Ratios: Low, 6.92/13.84; Intermediate, 4.2/8.4; Top, 2.88/5.76; Reverse, 5.76/11.52. Gear selector lever operates in quadrant on gearbox tunnel. Hardy Spicer needle bearing propeller shaft. Hypoid rear axle. Ratio, 2.88 : 1.

SUSPENSION—FRONT. Independent front suspension incorporating transverse wishbones and torsion bars controlled by telescopic hydraulic dampers. Anti-roll bar fitted to lower wishbones.

SUSPENSION—REAR. Fully independent rear suspension incorporating, on each side, a lower transverse tubular link pivoted at the rear wheel carrier and subframe adjacent to the differential case and, above this, a halfshaft universally jointed at each end. These serve to locate the wheel in a transverse plane. Longitudinal location is provided by the rubber mountings locating the sub-assembly in the body structure and by a radius arm between the lower link and a mounting point on the body structure. Twin coil high rate springs, each enclosing a telescopic damper, provide the suspension medium. The whole assembly together with the differential unit is carried in an easily detachable sub-frame which is located in the body structure by rubber mountings.

BRAKES. Dunlop bridge-type disc brakes featuring quick-change pads, are fitted to all four wheels. Front brakes fitted on wheel hubs, rear brakes fitted inboard of halfshafts adjacent to differential unit. Suspended vacuum type servo operated by tandem master cylinder. System divided into two entirely independent hydraulic circuits to front and rear brakes. Centrally positioned handbrake operates on rear wheels only. Combined handbrake and brake fluid warning light on Facia.

STEEERING. Rack and pinion. 16″ diameter steering wheel with separate adjustment for height and reach. Number of turns lock to lock, 2.85. Turning circle, 41 ft. diameter.

WHEELS AND TYRES. Wire spoke wheels with centre lock hubs. Dunlop 185 mm. by 15 ins. tyres with tubes.

FUEL SUPPLY. By S.U. electric pump. Tank of 14 imperial gallons capacity. Petrol Filter incorporated into fuel line and located in engine compartment.

ELECTRICAL EQUIPMENT, INSTRUMENTS AND FITTINGS. Lucas alternator. 12-volt negative earth system. Large capacity battery giving 57 amp.-hours at 10-hour rate with current voltage control. Eight fuse control box, fully labelled, located behind hinged central Facia panel for ease of access. Side lamps. Lucas sealed beam, asymmetric dip, headlamps with hand-operated dipping control on Facia. Separate lever actuating headlamp flashing and flashing direction indicators with self-cancellation. Direction indicator warning light on Facia. Separate stop-tail, direction and reflector units mounted in single assembly. Rear number plate lamps. Reversing light. Instruments and labelled switches illuminated by internal flood lighting controlled by a two-position dimmer switch. Interior light. Map reading light. Cigar lighter with luminous socket. 5 ins. diameter 160 m.p.h. speedometer incorporating total and trip distance recorders. 5 ins. diameter electrically operated revolution counter incorporating an electric clock. Ammeter. Electrically operated water temperature gauge, oil pressure gauge, fuel gauge with low level warning light. Choke warning light. Combined handbrake and brake fluid low level warning light. Twin blended-note horns. Triple blade two-speed self parking windscreen wiper unit. Electrically operated winscreen washers. Starter motor. Vacuum and centrifugal automatic ignition control. Oil coil ignition. Wiring harness in quickly detachable front body section connected to main circuits through an eight-pin connector mounted on engine compartment bulkhead.

BODY. Stressed shell steel body of unique, patented, monocoque construction. Front sub-frame of high tensile steel tubing carries engine unit, suspension and forward hinged front section. Counterbalanced, forward opening front section provides excellent accessibility to all mechanical components. Deep wrapround windscreen and thin pillars provide superb forward visibility. Wrapround bumpers with overriders at front and rear. Seating for four persons is fully upholstered in finest quality Vaumol leather over Dunlopillo foam rubber cushions. Twin bucket seats at the front have combined height and reach adjustment. Top section of rear seat squab moves forward allowing boot floor to be extended when car is used as two-seater, thus increasing luggage accommodation by 25%. Low floorline gives increased footroom in rear compartment. Three panel facia and screenrail in matt grained finish to eliminate reflection. Comprehensive instrumentation with revolution counter and speedometer positioned in front of driver. Central panel contains separate fuel, oil, water temperature gauges and ammeter together with row of labelled tumbler switches controlling ancillary equipment. Separate housing beneath panel contains radio and twin speakers (optional extra) together with ashtray. When no radio is fitted, speaker grilles are retained but radio control aperture is blanked off with an escutcheon. Panel in front of passenger contains lockable glove compartment and a grab handle. Full width parcel shelf. Three-spoke, polished alloy, lightweight steering wheel with wood rim and central horn push. Wide angle vertically adjustable rear view mirror incorporating anti-dazzle secondary mirror position. Sun visors. Deep pile carpets over thick felt underlay. Boot lid controlled from inside car.

HEATING AND DEMISTING. Fresh air heating system capable of high temperature and volume also gives rapid defrosting and demisting of windscreen. Variable direction nozzles are controlled individually by the front seat occupants. Controls are mounted each side of centre facia panel.

SPARE WHEEL AND TOOLS. The spare wheel is carried beneath the boot floor in a separate compartment and is readily accessible. The tools, in a fitted and lined container, are housed in the spare wheel compartment.

JACKING. Four point jacking allows individual wheel raising. Special studs, adjacent to each wheel, locate in forked lifting pad on screw type, manually-operated, easy lift jack.

PRINCIPAL DIMENSIONS. Wheelbase, 8 ft. 9 ins. Track, front and rear, 4 ft. 2 ins. Overall length, 15 ft. 4½ ins. Overall width, 5 ft. 5¼ ins. Overall height, 4 ft. 2 ins. Ground clearance (laden), 5½ ins. Dry weight (approx.) 22½ cwt.

JAGUAR 'E' TYPE 2+2 DIMENSIONS

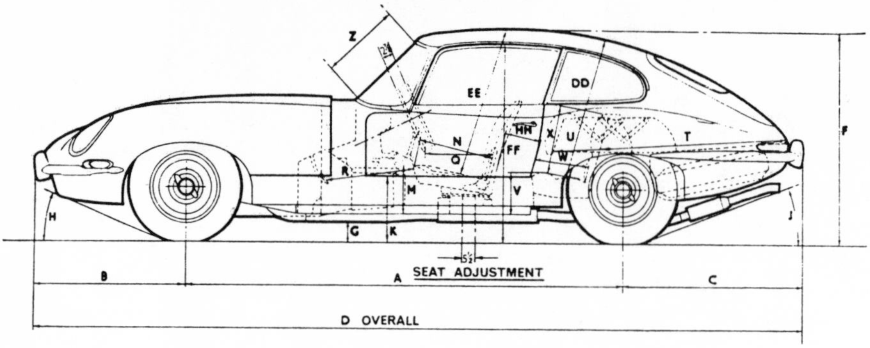

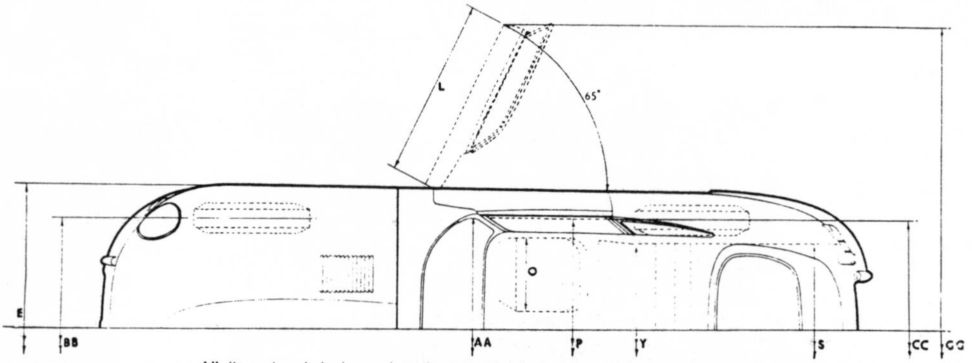

All dimensions in inches and centimetres unless otherwise stated and apply to a laden car.
NOTE: Front seat shown in mid position (5½" adjustment). Seats in unladen position.

		English	Metric			English	Metric
A	Wheelbase	105	267	S	Maximum Trunk Width	39	99
B	Front Overhang	36¼	92	T	Minimum Trunk Length	42	106
C	Rear Overhang	43⅛	109	U	Maximum Trunk Length	52½	133
D	Overall Length	184⅜	468	V	Rear Seat Height	9	23
E	Overall Width	65¼	166	W	Rear Seat Depth	14	36
F	Overall Height	50⅛	127	X	Rear Squab Height	17	43
G	Ground Clearance	5½	14	Y	Rear Squab Width	41	104
H	Front Clearance Angle	21°	21°	Z	Windscreen Depth	18⅛	46
J	Rear Clearance Angle	21°	21°	AA	Windscreen Width	50	128
K	Door Step Height	16	41	BB	Front Track	50	128
L	Door Opening	40½	102	CC	Rear Track	50	128
M	Front Seat Height	11	27	DD	Rear Headroom	33	84
N	Front Seat Depth	20	51	EE	Front Headroom	35½	90
O	Front Seat Width	18½	47	FF	Ground to Top of Door	46½	117
P	Shoulder Room	49	124	GG	O/A Width with Doors Fully Open	134	340
Q	Steering Wheel to Seat Squab	20	51				
R	Pedals to Cushion	19	48	HH	Knee Room (Rear)	8—10½	20—26

Jaguar 4.2 XK-E Coupe, Roadster & 2+2 Family Coupe

"A different breed of cat"

A combination of proved and technically superior features inherited from the famed D-type competition cars is the background for the latest 4.2 Jaguar XKE models ■ *Main Features:* Lightweight, strong mono-coque all steel body. Four-wheel independent suspension. Four-wheel disc brakes, with independent systems for front and rear. Quick, responsive rack and pinion steering ■ *New Features:* Larger, more powerful engine 4.2 litres capacity and 265 bhp. New, all synchromesh four speed gearbox, with hydraulically operated diaphragm clutch. More comfortable, fully padded individual seats. New alternator, new radiator.

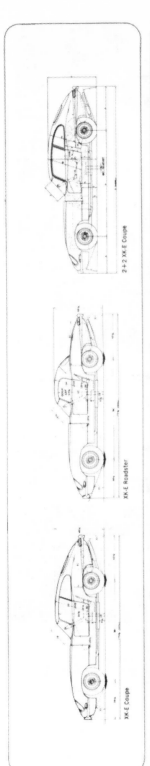

2+2 XK-E Coupe

XK-E Roadster

XK-E Coupe

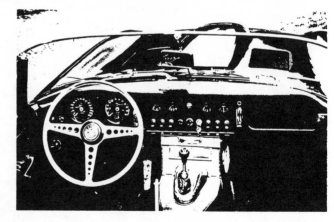

JAGUAR
4.2 LITRE
E-TYPE
SPORTS ROADSTER

ENGINE. Six cylinder 4.2 litre 'XK' engine with twin overhead camshafts and three carburetors. 3.63 bore × 4.17 stroke. Displacement, 4,235 c.c., 258.4 cu. ins., 265 b.h.p. at 5,400 r.p.m. Compression ratio 9 to 1. Pressurized cooling system with thermostatically controlled, electrically driven fan.

TRANSMISSION. Manually operated four-speed all-synchromesh gearbox.

SUSPENSION. (Front) Independent suspension – transverse wishbones and torsion bars and telescopic hydraulic dampers. (Rear) Fully independent suspension incorporating, on each side, a lower transverse tubular link pivoted at wheel carrier and subframe adjacent to differential case and, above this, a half-shaft universally jointed at each end. Twin coil springs at each road wheel, each enclose a telescopic damper.

BRAKES. Self-adjusting servo-assisted disc brakes all round. Independent hydraulic circuits to front and rear brakes.

STEERING. Rack and pinion steering. 2½ turns lock to lock. Turning circle 37 ft.

WHEELS & TIRES. Wire spoke wheels with centre lock hubs. Dunlop high performance tires.

FUEL SUPPLY. 16¾ gallon capacity tank. S.U. electric pump.

ELECTRICAL EQUIPMENT & INSTRUMENTS. Alternator. 12-volt battery with negative earth system. Pre-engaged starter motor. Extensive standard equipment includes sealed beam headlamps and headlamp flashing unit, map reading lamp, reversing lamp, triple blade two-speed windshield wipers, windshield washers, cigar lighter and comprehensive instrumentation to Jaguar normal high standards.

BODY. Stressed steel two-door two-seater body of monocoque construction. Folding hood with large rear window. (Hard top available as optional extra.) Twin bucket seats upholstered in finest quality leather hide over deep Dunlopillo cushions. Deep pile carpets over thick felt underlay. Seat belt anchorages incorporated.

HEATING & DEMISTING. High output fresh air heating and multi-point windscreen demisting system. Ducts direct air to each side of car. Two-speed fan.

SPARE WHEEL & TOOLS. Spare wheel housed beneath luggage boot floor. Comprehensive set of tools. Screw-type easy-lift jack.

PRINCIPAL DIMENSIONS. Wheelbase 96 ins., track front and rear 50 ins., overall length 175¼ ins., overall width 65¼ ins., overall height 46½ ins. Dry Weight, 2,464 lbs.

ENGINE. Six cylinder 4.2 litre 'XK' engine with twin overhead camshafts and three carburetors. 3.63 bore × 4.17 stroke. Capacity 4,235 c.c. 258.4 cu. ins., 265 b.h.p. at 5,400 r.p.m. Compression ratio 9 to 1 Pressurised cooling system with thermostatically controlled, electrically driven fan.

TRANSMISSION. Manually operated four-speed all-synchromesh gearbox.

SUSPENSION. (Front) Independent suspension – transverse wishbones and torsion bars and telescopic hydraulic dampers. (Rear) Fully Independent suspension incorporating, on each side, a lower transverse tubular link pivoted at wheel carrier and subframe adjacent to differential case and, above this, a half-shaft universally jointed at each end. Twin coil springs at each road wheel, each enclose a telescopic damper.

BRAKES. Self-adjusting servo-assisted disc brakes all round. Independent hydraulic circuits to front and rear brakes.

STEERING. Rack and pinion steering. 2½ turns lock to lock. Turning circle 37 ft.

WHEELS & TIRES. Wire spoke wheels with centre lock hubs. Dunlop high performance tires.

FUEL SUPPLY. 16¼ gallon capacity tank. S.U. electric pump.

ELECTRICAL EQUIPMENT & INSTRUMENTS. Alternator. 12-volt battery with negative earth system. Pre-engaged starter motor. Extensive standard equipment includes sealed beam headlamps and headlamp flashing unit, map reading lamp, reversing lamp, triple blade two-speed windshield wipers, windshield washers, cigar lighter and comprehensive instrumentation to Jaguar normal high standards.

BODY. Stressed steel two-door two-seater body of monocoque construction. Twin bucket seats upholstered in first quality leather hide over deep Dunlopillo cushions. Deep pile carpets over thick felt underlay. Seat belt anchorages incorporated.

HEATING & DEMISTING. High output fresh air heating and multi-point windscreen demisting system. Ducts direct air to each side of car. Two-speed fan.

SPARE WHEEL & TOOLS. Spare wheel housed beneath luggage boot floor. Comprehensive set of tools. Screw-type easy-lift jack.

PRINCIPAL DIMENSIONS. Wheelbase 96 ins. track front and rear 50 ins., overall length 175¼ ins., overall width 65¼ ins., overall height 48 ins. Dry Weight, 2,520 lbs.

JAGUAR
4.2 LITRE
E-TYPE
HARD TOP COUPE

JAGUAR

4.2 LITRE

E-TYPE 2+2

FAMILY COUPE

ENGINE. Six cylinder 4.2 litre 'XK' engine with twin overhead camshafts and three carburetors. 3.63 ins. bore × 4.17 ins. stroke. Displacement 4,235 c.c., 258.4 cu ins. 265 b.h.p. at 5,400 r.p.m. Compression ratio 9 to 1. Pressurised cooling system with thermostatically controlled electric fan.

TRANSMISSION. (Manual) Four-speed all-synchromesh gearbox. Centrally positioned gear change lever. (Automatic) Borg Warner Model 8 with dual drive range D1/D2. Selector level operates in quadrant on gearbox tunnel.

SUSPENSION. (Front) Independent by transverse wishbones and torsion bars with telescopic hydraulic dampers. (Rear) Fully independent, having on each side, a lower transverse tubular link pivoted at the rear wheel carrier and subframe adjacent to differential case and, above this, a half-shaft universally jointed at each end. Twin coil springs at each road wheel, each enclose a telescopic damper.

BRAKES. Self-adjusting servo-assisted disc brakes all round. Independent hydraulic circuit to front and rear brakes.

STEERING. Rack and pinion steering. 2.85 turns lock to lock. Turning circle 41 ft.

WHEELS & TIRES. Wire spoke wheels with centre lock hubs. Dunlop high performance tires.

FUEL SUPPLY. 16¾ gallons capacity tank. S.U. electric pump.

ELECTRICAL EQUIPMENT & INSTRUMENTS. Alternator. 12-volt battery with negative earth system. Pre-engaged starter motor. Extensive standard equipment includes sealed beam headlamps and headlamp flashing unit, reversing lamp, map reading lamp, cigar lighter, triple-blade two-speed windshield wiper, windshield washers, and comprehensive instrumentation to Jaguar normal high standards.

BODY. Two-door, stressed steel monocoque body incorporating four seats fully upholstered in finest quality leather hide over deep Dunlopillo cushions. Top section of rear seat squab moves forward, extending floor to give 25% more luggage space when car is used as two-seater. Deep pile carpets over thick underlay. Seat belt anchorages incorporated.

HEATING & DEMISTING. High output fresh air heating system gives rapid defrosting and demisting of windscreen. Variable direction nozzles controlled individually by front seat occupants.

SPARE WHEEL & TOOLS. Spare wheel housed beneath boot floor. Comprehensive set of tools. Screw type easy-lift jack.

PRINCIPAL DIMENSIONS. Wheelbase 105 ins., track front and rear 50 ins., overall length 184½ ins., overall width 65¼ ins., overall height 50 ins. Dry Weight, 2,772 lbs.

JAGUAR

COUPE

S-E COUPE
(optional automatic)

JAGUAR ROADSTER 2+2

Development of the E-type: The Ultimate in Jaguar Sports Cars

Fundamentally the Jaguar car is the concept of one man, William Lyons. He founded his manufacturing company in 1921 and within ten years developed it from the fabrication of motorcycle sidecars and special coachwork on small sports cars, into a significant place among English car manufacturers. Then during the next thirty years, he and his principal colleagues built Jaguar into one of the most prestigious and successful makes of car the world has known.

The entire progression of Jaguar cars across more than 35 years reflects the genius and taste of William Lyons. Graceful fender lines. Striking arrangement of head, side and auxiliary lights. Long engine covers and always rounded curves of carefully calculated proportion. Jaguars have consistently been winners of Concours d'Elegance. They have been remarkable not only for their appearance but also for outstanding performance, and finally for value for money. The E-type combines all these qualities to a supreme degree.

Coachbuilding Beginnings

William Lyons' original company in Blackpool, Lancashire, was called the Swallow Sidecar Company and produced special versions of popular makes of car, such as the Standard Swallow on a chassis by the Standard Motor Company. It was from this model that the company derived its name, S. S. Cars Limited, when it was formed into a public company in 1934.

The first SS car had astonished the motoring world at the annual London motor show in the fall of 1931. It was a sports coupe with somewhat exaggerated length of hood (or bonnet as it is called in England), a fashionable trend at the time. It gained immediate fame, and later versions of this the SS 1, up to 1935, were refined into some of the best looking cars of their day. In 1933 the company made its first ventures into the severe world of competitive motor sport and some success was enjoyed in the International Alpine Trials of that year.

In 1936 an equal sensation was caused by the introduction of the SS 100 two-seater, the company's highest performance sports car to date and one which has deservedly become a classic. The SS 100 was all works (2½ or 3½ litre overhead valve Six, giving up to 125 b.h.p. in standard form and reaching 120 mph in racing form). There was the minimum space for driver, passenger and luggage, and comfort was somewhat sacrificed to speed. In British rallies in 1937, the SS 100 swept the board.

The First 'Jaguar' Model

At the same time as this new emphasis on sports cars, the SS Jaguar 2½ litre sedan was announced in 1936, actually the first to be called a Jaguar. It offered fantastic value, since it provided a car frankly reminiscent of the most expensive luxury cars of those times but at a third of their cost. The company's fortunes soared and production was boosted to a full range of five models.

The end of World War II—during which the Coventry factory, converted to aircraft component production, had been severely bombed—brought Jaguar engineers an opportunity to experiment with an important new power unit termed the XK.

Then came the surprise announcement in 1948 of this the first really post-war Jaguar, the great XK-120 series. By then (1945) the company's name had become Jaguar Cars Limited.

One of the World's Most Powerful Engines

For those days the XK 120 had one of the world's most powerful passenger car engines, a twin overhead camshaft Six, developing 160 bhp at 5000 rpm. The car's body was highly streamlined in contrast of the pre-war SS 100. The XK 120 became the outstanding sports car of the Fifties and thousands were welcomed by Americans. Many are still in circulation after fifteen years or so.

Responsible for the design was a team who still control Jaguar engineering today. They are led by William Heynes, now Deputy Chairman (Engineering). As to styling, this has always been and remains the sole province of William Lyons, in acknowledgement of which he received the title of Royal Designer for Industry.

Jaguar Takes to Racing

With many enthusiastic owners insisting on racing the XK 120, Jaguar soon found itself involved in its own competition program. In 1951 an outstanding sports racing model, the C-type was developed to win the Le Mans 24-hour Race, and succeeded. Between then and 1957, Jaguar cars won at Le Mans no fewer than five times, a performance for which the name of Jaguar must be forever famous in automobile history. Following this, the founder of the company was knighted by Queen Elizabeth II and became Sir William Lyons, in token of his contribution to British industry.

The 2000-mile Le Mans endurance race left its mark permanently on the qualities of the Jaguar car, which offers tremendous reserves of effortless power and tireless fast cruising. For Le Mans was created the wonderful D-type sports/racing car of 1954. This soon evolved into even more powerful and speedier versions. The engine size, starting as it did with the original XK 120 of 3.4 litres, grew to 3.8 litres. Fuel injection and four-wheel independent suspension were added, until D-types achieved up to 200 mph on the road circuits.

Production Expanded by Acquisition

In the early Sixties, Jaguar expanded substantially as a manufacturing organization. The need to increase production and diversify encouraged the acquisition of such famous companies as Daimler cars (1960), Guy trucks (1961), Coventry Climax engines (1963) and Henry Meadows engines (1965).

Announcement of the First XK-E

The XK 120 series had grown through XK 140 and XK 150 models. Following the racing D-type came a road edition, the XK SS of 1957, a really rugged 160 mph sports racing car with full traffic equipment. Finally in 1961 came another automobile landmark for Jaguar, the first XKE or E-type, a 3.8 litre.

From that first example derived the complete line of more powerful, more refined E-types of today—the 4.2 litre roadster, coupe and 2 + 2 models.

(Key to car photos: inside back cover)

XK-E TYPE COUPE

"Fundamentally the Jaguar car is the concept of one man ..."

Sir William Lyons, R.D.I., Royal Designer for Industry
Founder, Chairman and Managing Director of Jaguar Cars
Limited of Coventry, Warwickshire, England.

(Knight Bachelor created 1956, by Her Majesty Queen Elizabeth II, for services
to British industry and exports, following the long line of Jaguar car successes in
international motor races and maintenance of Jaguar car exports in excess
of half of total production.)

Engineering Eminence and Styling Comfort

In these pictures are seen not only the beauty but also the engineering eminence and styling comfort, which makeup the unrivalled reputation of the Jaguar E-type. To meet U.S. federal traffic safety regulations, Jaguar has developed new styling features. These include new type headlights, with attractive painted and chromium-plated surrounds. The interior handles are countersunk deep into the base of the wide doors. Wire wheels have 'earless' hub caps removable with a special spanner.

Advanced Technical Specifications

The acknowledged superiority of Jaguar car performance derives principally from the durability and adaptability of the power unit. The twin-overhead camshaft layout for double overhead valve operation, plus hemispherical combustion chambers, gives noted built-in efficiency. Standard equipment includes alternator, oil coil ignition and thermostatically controlled twin electric cooling fans.

Jaguar has designed a new Duplex Manifold to meet U.S. federal air pollution regulations. Simple, efficient and requiring the minimum of service, it not only reduces exhaust emissions as required by law but brings improved engine flexibility and torque at lower traffic speeds. The induction manifold is connected to the exhaust manifold by a polished Duplex Manifold, which pre-heats the fuel gases before they enter the combustion chambers. Jaguar's great XK-E power-unit retains its handsome appearance and includes new, louvred camshaft covers.

The XK engine, in its various forms according to model, always develops well in excess of 200 brake horse power. It drives the rear wheels through a close-ratio, all-synchromesh, four-speed transmission. The rear wheels take the drive through Jaguar's own design of independent suspension using two coil springs enclosing hydraulic dampers, to each wheel.

Styling Changes and New Appointments

In making styling changes to meet the U.S. safety regulations, Jaguar has further improved the convenience and appointments of the luxury E-type sports cars. All switches, including the hazard warning system, are now grouped together centrally, clearly marked and of rocker-type. Separate transistorized clock and battery condition indicator are included. New flush fitting heater and choke controls, and newly located cigarette lighter and console ashtray are other features.

When the top is down on the roadster, it is neatly concealed beneath the rear deck and reveals the interesting, fully instrumented cockpit. There are reclining, individually adjustable, bucket seats of genuine leather upholstery over deep foam rubber. The spring-spoked wood-rimmed steering wheel has a telescopically adjustable column, of breakaway type. There is a surprising amount of luggage space, locked by internal release, which raises the deck lid.

The E-type represents the culmination of all Jaguar's long experience of building quality, performance cars. The construction of stressed skin body/frame is taken direct from the D-type racing car. The four-wheel independent suspension was also race-proved on that model. Jaguar alone of the world's car manufacturers developed by racing, then pioneered production of, four-wheel disc brakes, which now are being adopted on all cars.

COUPE

Two Coupe Styles Offered
The E-type line includes two beautiful coupe models. The 2 + 2, with 9 inch longer wheelbase, offers a fully upholstered rear seat for children.
It is also the only E-type model available with automatic transmission. A great performance car but with space for the family.

All E-types have 72-spoke wire wheels as standard equipment, with full chromium plating as optional extra. Also standard are the latest high performance radial-ply tires, which bring improved road grip, directional stability, tread wear and even gas mileage. They run cooler and smoother.

Generous Luggage Space
The coupes have large luggage space, reached through a hinged rear window. This window can be electrically heated through an invisible wire mesh to demist and defrost. It is opened by a safety catch on the inside of the car. The luggage deck on the standard coupe can be folded back to provide parcel space behind the seats. Jaguar's lighting meets the latest regulations and incorporates an extra lever on the steering column actuating headlamp flashing. Wrap-around parking and signal lights are installed above complete steel bumpers, which stretch from wheel arch to wheel arch on all models.

With its enlarged passenger and luggage accommodation, and with optional automatic transmission, the 2 + 2 now appeals to an even larger number of women drivers. The rear seat doubles as a fold-down luggage platform, giving capacity 52½ in. in length.

Impressive Range of Performance
E-types have tremendous performance which compares with any other sports car. Acceleration from 0 to 60 mph takes less than 8 seconds. 90 miles an hour can be reached in just over the quarter mile. 100 mph takes about 18 seconds. The car speeds as high as 140 mph. Yet with all this, gas mileage at a constant 60 mph exceeds 20 miles to the gallon. All this is achieved by a combination of the E-type's high power-to-weight ratio, with highly efficient streamline form.

Experts Hail the E-type
A scale model of the beautiful XKE coupe forms part of the permanent collection of New York's Museum of Modern Art.

The Museum commented: "It offers a standard of performance and finish found only in cars normally costing twice as much money."

Says Road and Track magazine of the XKE: "It still has a combination of ride, handling and silence that sets the standard for the rest of the world."

2 + 2 COUPE

Bring Home A Jaguar From Your Trip Abroad

The Jaguar Overseas Delivery Plan (JOD. PLAN) brings great advantages to the customer who buys his car this way. A Jaguar may be purchased at any of some 300 dealer points throughout North America for immediate delivery. But also, any of those same dealerships can arrange to effect delivery overseas

For instance, tourists visiting Britain and the Continent of Europe can purchase Jaguar cars at special low tax free prices. This applies whether their visit is for a carefree touring holiday or for business. The same principle applies to members of the Armed Forces on duty overseas, who on returning to the U.S. can arrange to have a new Jaguar waiting stateside.

For the international traveler and especially for the international businessman there are manifold advantages and pleasures in having one's own car, while traveling through the beautiful British Isles and on the Continent.

Not only is there the luxurious convenience of one's own Jaguar when motoring in other countries but substantial savings can be achieved as well. First there is the saving on the original price of the car, because it is bought at the tax free ex-factory price. Then there is the saving during the tour on car rental or on intermediate train and rail fares, not to speak of taxis. You will be completely free to go where you want, when you want and stay as long as you like.

Finally, when the car is shipped back home, a reduced import duty assessment is incurred on the used car value.

Easy Arrangements Under The Jaguar Plan

Special arrangements have been made to avoid red tape, whether delivery is made in Britain, France, Italy or any other major European country. Inclusive prices, plus delivery charges, will be confirmed by the Jaguar dealer. Each car is ordered individually to the exact color and optional equipment of the customer's choice. Each car is to correct North American specification, including all the latest traffic safety and air pollution requirements.

Your Own Jaguar for a Holiday in Europe

Therefore, your very own choice of Jaguar can be ready and waiting for you the day of your arrival, so that no time is lost in starting the tour abroad. However, normally at least eight weeks notice is requested. Rush orders can be accepted and met, from stock car orders.

All that is necessary is a visit to your nearest Jaguar dealer to select the exact model, and colors for the exterior and interior of the car. Make sure you buy through the American or Canadian dealer to whom you will be going for future service. He will give you a demonstration drive, and register your order with the manufacturer. Payment is normally arranged with a small deposit and full payment 30 days before delivery.

Documentation has been reduced to a minimum. For Britain, car purchase order form and purchase tax exemption form (in duplicate). Both will be completed by the dealer. For the Continent, car purchase order form and Power of Attorney form (in duplicate), necessary to speed car registration in advance of arrival.

Take Delivery In Any Major City

Delivery charges vary according to the country and city chosen, and the distance from the Jaguar factory in Coventry, England. Charges range for example from Coventry itself ($40), London ($57), Paris ($186) to Rome ($362). These charges include delivery by bonded bi-lingual drivers; license plates; and associate membership in the Royal Automobile Club, which has representatives at all major ports and cities. Current American driver's license covers you in most countries.

Jaguar enthusiasts often prefer to take delivery at the Coventry factory itself, where they see how Jaguar cars are built, inspected and tested and have the opportunity to visit the surrounding Shakespeare country; besides saving on delivery charges.

Airport or dockside deliveries are not necessarily recommended due to the uncertainties of late or even early arrivals. But such deliveries can be arranged at an extra charge from $15 to $25 in the U.K.

Car insurance is compulsory abroad and can be arranged through the International Department of the American Automobile Association. It is necessary to list all the countries to be visited.

Arrangements For Shipping The Car Home

Return shipment is easily arranged and instructions can be confirmed before actually leaving the U.S.A., through the Jaguar shipping agents Dunnington and Arnold, 21 West Street, New York, N. Y. 10006; or when taking delivery abroad through the Jaguar factory representative or through a shipping agent. The RAC have a complete list. Shipping and marine insurance charges are for the account of the purchaser.

If shipping arrangements have to be made later this can also be accomplished quite simply in any major port or city, by leaving your car with an automobile forwarding agency who will arrange shipment of the car to the U.S.A.

In Britain the car can be left with the Jaguar London shipping agents or at the factory itself in Coventry. It is then shipped to the U.S.A. with other new Jaguars under factory supervision. Cost varies according to model and ports, from about $256 from England to East Coast U.S.A.

ENGINE. Six cylinder 4·2 litre 'XK' engine with twin overhead camshafts and three carburetters. 92·07 mm. bore × 106 mm. stroke. Capacity 4,235 c.c., 265 b.h.p. at 5,400 r.p.m. Compression ratio 9 to 1 (8 to 1 optional). Pressurised cooling system with thermostatically controlled, electrically driven fan.

TRANSMISSION. Manually operated four-speed all-synchromesh gearbox.

SUSPENSION. (Front) Independent suspension—transverse wishbones and torsion bars and telescopic hydraulic dampers. (Rear) Fully independent suspension incorporating, on each side, a lower transverse tubular link pivoted at wheel carrier and subframe adjacent to differential case and, above this, a half-shaft universally jointed at each end. Twin coil springs each enclose a telescopic damper.

BRAKES. Servo-assisted disc brakes all round. Independent hydraulic circuits to front and rear brakes.

STEERING. Rack and pinion steering. 2½ turns lock to lock.

WHEELS & TYRES. Wire spoke wheels with centre lock hubs. Dunlop 185 mm. × 15 ins. SP41 HR tyres and tubes.

FUEL SUPPLY. 14 Imperial gallon capacity tank. S.U. electric pump.

ELECTRICAL EQUIPMENT & INSTRUMENTS. Alternator generator. 12-volt battery with negative earth system. Pre-engaged starter motor. Extensive standard equipment includes sealed beam headlamps and headlamp flashing unit, map reading lamp, reversing lamp, triple blade two-speed windscreen wipers, windscreen washers, cigar lighter, automatic ignition advance and comprehensive instrumentation to Jaguar normal high standards.

BODY. Stressed steel two-door two-seater body of monocoque construction. Folding hood with large rear window. (Hard top available as optional extra.) Twin bucket seats upholstered in finest quality leather hide over deep Dunlopillo cushions. Deep pile carpets over thick felt underlay.

HEATING & DEMISTING. High output fresh air heating and multi-point windscreen demisting system. Ducts direct air to each side of car. Two-speed fan.

SPARE WHEEL & TOOLS. Spare wheel housed beneath boot floor. Comprehensive set of tools in fitted and lined container. Screw-type easy-lift jack.

PRINCIPAL DIMENSIONS. Wheelbase 8 ft., track front and rear 4 ft. 2 ins., overall length 14 ft. 7 7/16 ins., overall width 5 ft. 5¼ ins., overall height 4 ft., turning circle 37 ft.

ENGINE. Six cylinder 4·2 litre 'XK' engine with twin overhead camshafts and three carburetters. 92·07 mm. bore × 106 mm. stroke. Capacity 4,235 c.c., 265 b.h.p. at 5,400 r.p.m. Compression ratio 9 to 1 (8 to 1 optional). Pressurised cooling system with thermostatically controlled, electrically driven fan.

TRANSMISSION. Manually operated four-speed all-synchromesh gearbox.

SUSPENSION. (Front) Independent suspension—transverse wishbones and torsion bars and telescopic hydraulic dampers. (Rear) Fully independent suspension incorporating, on each side, a lower transverse tubular link pivoted at wheel carrier and subframe adjacent to differential case and, above this, a half-shaft universally jointed at each end. Twin coil springs each enclose a telescopic damper.

BRAKES. Servo-assisted disc brakes all round. Independent hydraulic circuits to front and rear brakes.

STEERING. Rack and pinion steering. 2⅝ turns lock to lock.

WHEELS & TYRES. Wire spoke wheels with centre lock hubs. Dunlop 185 mm. × 15 ins. SP41 HR tyres and tubes.

FUEL SUPPLY. 14 Imperial gallon capacity tank. S.U. electric pump.

ELECTRICAL EQUIPMENT & INSTRUMENTS. Alternator generator. 12-volt battery with negative earth system. Pre-engaged starter motor. Extensive standard equipment includes sealed beam headlamps and headlamp flashing unit, map reading lamp, reversing lamp, triple blade two-speed windscreen wipers, windscreen washers, cigar lighter, automatic ignition advance, and comprehensive instrumentation to Jaguar normal high standards.

BODY. Stressed steel two-door two-seater body of monocoque construction. Twin bucket seats upholstered in finest quality leather hide over deep Dunlopillo cushions. Deep pile carpets over thick felt underlay.

HEATING & DEMISTING. High output fresh air heating and multi-point windscreen demisting system. Ducts direct air to each side of car. Two-speed fan.

SPARE WHEEL & TOOLS. Spare wheel housed beneath boot floor. Comprehensive set of tools in fitted and lined container. Screw-type easy-lift jack.

PRINCIPAL DIMENSIONS. Wheelbase 8 ft., track front and rear 4 ft. 2 ins., overall length 14 ft. 7 7/16 ins., overall width 5 ft. 5¼ ins., overall height 4 ft., turning circle 37 ft.

ENGINE. Six cylinder 4·2 litre 'XK' engine with twin overhead camshafts and three carburetters. 92·07 mm. bore × 106 mm. stroke. Capacity 4,235 c.c., 265 b.h.p. at 5,400 r.p.m. Compression ratio 9 to 1 (8 to 1 optional). Pressurised cooling system with thermostatically controlled electric fan.

TRANSMISSION. (Manual) Four-speed all-synchromesh gearbox. Centrally positioned gear change lever. (Automatic) Borg Warner Model 8 with dual drive range D1/D2. Selector lever operates in quadrant on gearbox tunnel.

SUSPENSION. (Front) Independent by transverse wishbones and torsion bars with telescopic hydraulic dampers. (Rear) Fully independent, having, on each side, a lower transverse tubular link pivoted at the rear wheel carrier and subframe adjacent to differential case and, above this, a half-shaft universally jointed at each end. Twin coil springs each enclose a telescopic damper.

BRAKES. Servo-assisted disc brakes all round. Independent hydraulic circuits to front and rear brakes.

STEERING. Rack and pinion steering. 2·85 turns lock to lock.

WHEELS & TYRES. Wire spoke wheels with centre lock hubs. Dunlop 185 mm. × 15 ins. SP41 HR tyres and tubes.

FUEL SUPPLY. 14 Imperial gallons capacity tank. S.U. electric pump.

ELECTRICAL EQUIPMENT & INSTRUMENTS. Alternator generator. 12-volt battery with negative earth system. Pre-engaged starter motor. Extensive standard equipment includes sealed beam headlamps and headlamp flashing unit, reversing lamp, map reading lamp, cigar lighter, automatic ignition advance, triple-blade two-speed windscreen wiper, windscreen washers, and comprehensive instrumentation to Jaguar normal high standards.

BODY. Two-door, stressed steel monocoque body incorporating four seats fully upholstered in finest quality leather hide over deep Dunlopillo cushions. Top section of rear seat squab moves forward, extending boot floor to give 25% more luggage space when car is used as two-seater. Deep pile carpets over thick underlay.

HEATING & DEMISTING. High output fresh air heating system gives rapid defrosting and demisting of windscreen. Variable direction nozzles controlled individually by front seat occupants.

SPARE WHEEL & TOOLS. Spare wheel housed beneath boot floor. Comprehensive set of tools in fitted and lined container. Screw type easy-lift jack.

PRINCIPAL DIMENSIONS. Wheelbase 8 ft. 9 ins., track front and rear 4 ft. 2 ins., overall length 15 ft. 4½ ins., overall width 5 ft. 5½ ins., overall height 4 ft. 2 ins., turning circle 41 ft.

4.2 Liter Series II

Throughout its entire production life the XK-E was targeted at the U.S. market. Consequently, when the U.S. government mandated regulations for exhaust emissions and safety devices, Jaguar paid heed. Unlike many low volume European manufacturers who abandoned the U.S. market, Jaguar had little choice but to comply. In the case of the XK-E, so many changes were wrought that a new series, the Series II 4.2 Liter, was designated.

The Series II bowed in the fall of 1968. With the two exceptions of the new Girling disc brakes and the availability of power steering, all of the changes reflected those required by the U.S. government. Exhaust emission requirements were met in stages in 1968, 1969 and 1970, but the changes relating to safety all came in the fall of 1968. Bumpers were raised. New larger taillamps were positions beneath the bumper. Side marker lights were added. The spinners were taken off the new wire wheels. Inside there was a snap-off mirror, locking seat backs, headrests and a collapsible steering column with lock. In short, everything General Motors, Ford and Chrysler had to do, Jaguar did as well.

The Series II 4.2 Liter was in production until early 1971 with 18,808 cars built in a little over two years. That's a yearly average of over 7,500 cars. This was significantly more than earlier XK-E production. The breakdown by body style was 8,627 roadsters, 4,855 two-passenger coupes and 5,326 2+2 coupes. The U.K. market still preferred the closed cars better than two to one. Americans were now buying XK-Es about half open and half closed.

The main British item on the Series II 4.2 Liter was a stiff paper folder. There was a small black-and-white full-line catalogue dated 10/68 (see pages 75-77) and a similar black-and-white folder. A Canadian color sheet (BLC 11) appears on page 78. American literature was more plentiful, headed by a handsome color catalogue on the XK-E models (see pages 79-83) and a similar folder that also included the new XJ6 sedan. A 1969 black-and-white overseas delivery folder is reproduced on pages 84-85. There was a similar folder without the overseas delivery information. The XK-E spread from a "Vogue" magazine catalogue appears on pages 86-87. There were several 1970 vintage items, including a large color catalogue that included the XJ6 sedan (see pages 88-92) and two similar folders. The 1971 literature consisted primarily of two large color cards (see page 93) and a black-and-white sheet (see page 94).

JAGUAR:
THE CAR THAT MAKES GREAT BRITAIN
A GREAT SPORTS CAR POWER
CAN MAKE YOU ONE TOO.

[FOR LESS THAN YOU THINK]

0-60 mph	6.7 sec.
0-100 mph	19.0 sec.
Standing 1/4 mile	15.3 sec.
Speed 1/4 mile	90 mph
Horsepower	245 bhp

Statistical Source: XK-E Roadster, Car and Driver, May, 1969

**FOR EXACT COMPARISONS [SPECIFICATIONS, PERFORMANCE, AND PRICE]
WITH OTHER GREAT SPORTS CAR POWERS, SEE YOUR JAGUAR DEALER.**

ENGINE. Six cylinder 4·2 litre 'XK' engine with twin overhead camshafts and three carburetters. 92·07 mm bore × 106 mm stroke. Capacity 4235 cc, 265 bhp at 5,400 rpm. Compression ratio 9 : 1 (8 : 1 optional). Cross flow radiator, "No loss" cooling system with thermostatically controlled, electrically driven twin fans.

TRANSMISSION. Manually operated four-speed all-synchromesh gearbox. Improved Helix angle for quieter running.

SUSPENSION. (Front) independent suspension—transverse wishbones and torsion bars and telescopic hydraulic dampers. (Rear) fully independent suspension incorporating, on each side, a lower transverse tubular link pivoted at wheel carrier and subframe adjacent to differential case and, above this, a half-shaft universally jointed at each end. Twin coil springs each enclose a telescopic damper.

BRAKES. Servo-assisted disc brakes all round. Independent hydraulic circuits to front and rear brakes.

STEERING. Rack and pinion steering. Collapsible steering column. 2¼ turns lock to lock. Power assisted steering optional extra.

WHEELS AND TYRES. Wire spoke wheels with centre lock hubs. Dunlop SP Sport tyres and tubes. Optional pressed-steel wheels available.

FUEL SUPPLY. 14 Imperial gallon capacity tank. S.U. electric pump.

ELECTRICAL EQUIPMENT AND INSTRUMENTS. Alternator generator. 12-volt battery with negative earth system. Pre-engaged starter motor. Extensive standard equipment includes sealed beam headlamps and headlamp flashing unit, map reading lamp, reversing lamps, flashing direction indicators doubling as hazard warning lights, triple blade two-speed windscreen wipers, windscreen washers, cigar lighter, transistorised clock, automatic ignition advance and comprehensive instrumentation to Jaguar normal high standards.

BODY. Stressed steel two-door two-seater body of monocoque construction. Folding hood with large rear window. (Hard top available as optional extra). Twin semi-reclining bucket seats upholstered in finest quality leather hide over deep Dunlopillo cushions. Deep pile carpets over thick felt underlay.

HEATING AND DEMISTING. High output fresh air heating and multipoint windscreen demisting system. Ducts direct air to each side of car. Two-speed fan.

SPARE WHEEL AND TOOLS. Spare wheel housed beneath boot floor. Comprehensive set of tools. Screw-type easy-lift jack.

PRINCIPAL DIMENSIONS. Wheelbase 8 ft., track front and rear 4 ft. 2 in., overall length 14 ft. 7⅞ in., overall width 5 ft. 5¼ in., overall height 4 ft. 0 in., turning circle 37 ft.

Jaguar 'E' Type
series 2
Open Two Seater

Jaguar 'E' Type
series 2
Fixed Head Coupé

ENGINE. Six cylinder 4·2 litre 'XK' engine with twin overhead camshafts and three carburetters. 92·07 mm bore × 106 mm stroke. Capacity 4235 cc, 265 bhp at 5,400 rpm. Compression ratio 9 : 1 (8 : 1 optional). Cross flow radiator, "No loss" cooling system with thermostatically controlled, electrically driven twin fans.

TRANSMISSION. Manually operated four-speed all-synchromesh gearbox. Improved Helix angle for quieter running.

SUSPENSION. (Front) independent suspension—transverse wishbones and torsion bars and telescopic hydraulic dampers. (Rear) fully independent suspension incorporating, on each side, a lower transverse tubular link pivoted at wheel carrier and subframe adjacent to differential case and, above this, a half-shaft universally jointed at each end. Twin coil springs each enclose a telescopic damper.

BRAKES. Servo-assisted disc brakes all round. Independent hydraulic circuits to front and rear brakes.

STEERING. Rack and pinion steering. Collapsible steering column. 2¼ turns lock to lock. Power assisted steering optional extra.

WHEELS AND TYRES. Wire spoke wheels with centre lock hubs. Dunlop 185 mm × 15 in. SP41 HR tyres and tubes. Optional pressed-steel wheels available.

FUEL SUPPLY. 14 Imperial gallon capacity tank. S.U. electric pump.

ELECTRICAL EQUIPMENT AND INSTRUMENTS. Alternator 12-volt battery with negative earth system. Pre-engaged starter motor. Extensive standard equipment includes sealed beam headlamps and headlamp flashing unit, map reading lamp, reversing lamps, flashing direction indicators doubling as hazard warning lights, triple-blade two-speed windscreen wipers, windscreen washers, cigar lighter, transistorised clock, and comprehensive instrumentation to Jaguar normal high standards.

BODY. Stressed steel two-door two-seater body of monocoque construction. Twin bucket seats upholstered in finest quality leather hide over deep Dunlopillo cushions. Deep pile carpets over thick felt underlay.

HEATING AND DEMISTING. High output fresh air heating and multi-point windscreen demisting system. Ducts direct air to each side of car. Two-speed fan.

SPARE WHEEL AND TOOLS. Spare wheel housed beneath boot floor. Comprehensive set of tools. Screw-type easy-lift jack.

PRINCIPAL DIMENSIONS. Wheelbase 8 ft. 0 in., track front and rear 4 ft. 2 in., overall length 14 ft. 7⅞ in., overall width 5 ft. 5¼ in., overall height 4 ft. 0 in., turning circle 37 ft.

Jaguar series 2 'E' Type 2 + 2 Fixed Head Coupé

ENGINE. Six cylinder 4·2 litre 'XK' engine with twin overhead camshafts and three carburetters. 92·07 mm bore × 106 mm stroke. Capacity 4235 cc, 265 bhp at 5,400 rpm. Compression ratio 9 : 1 (8 : 1 optional). Pressurised cooling system with thermostatically controlled twin electric fans.

TRANSMISSION. (Manual) four-speed all-synchromesh gearbox. Centrally positioned gear change lever. (Automatic) Borg Warner Model 8 with dual drive range, D1 /D2.

SUSPENSION. (Front) Independent by transverse wishbones and torsion bars with telescopic hydraulic dampers. (Rear) fully independent, having, on each side, a lower transverse tubular link pivoted at the rear wheel carrier and subframe adjacent to differential case and, above this, a half-shaft universally jointed at each end. Twin coil springs each enclose a telescopic damper.

BRAKES. Servo-assisted disc brakes all round. Independent hydraulic circuits to front and rear brakes.

STEERING. Rack and pinion steering 2·85 turns lock to lock. Collapsible steering column.

WHEELS AND TYRES. Wire spoke wheels with centre lock hubs. Dunlop SP Sport tyres and tubes. Optional pressed-steel wheels available.

FUEL SUPPLY. 14 Imperial gallons capacity tank. S.U. electric pump.

ELECTRIC EQUIPMENT AND INSTRUMENTS. Alternator, 12-volt battery with negative earth system. Pre-engaged starter motor. Extensive standard equipment includes sealed beam headlamps and head-lamp flashing unit, reversing lamps, map reading lamp, flashing direction indicators doubling as hazard warning lights, cigar lighter, twin-blade two-speed windscreen wiper. windscreen washers, transistorised clock and comprehensive instrumentation to Jaguar normal high standards.

BODY. Two-door, stressed steel monocoque body incorporating four seats fully upholstered in finest quality leather hide over deep Dunlopillo cushions. Top section of rear seat squab moves forward, extending boot floor to give 25% more luggage space when car is used as two-seater. Deep pile carpets over thick underlay.

HEATING AND DEMISTING. High output fresh air heating system gives rapid defrosting and demisting of windscreen. Variable direction nozzles controlled individually by front seat occupants.

SPARE WHEEL AND TOOLS. Spare wheel housed beneath boot floor. Comprehensive set of tools. Screw-type easy-lift jack.

PRINCIPAL DIMENSIONS. Wheelbase 8 ft. 9 in., track front and rear 4 ft. 2 in., overall length 15 ft. 4½ in., overall width 5 ft. 5¼ in., overall height 4 ft. 2 in., turning circle 41 ft.

XK-E 1969

The exceptional breeding provided by a competition background is evident in all aspects of the XK-E, and most dramatically in the layout of the cockpit. It is essential for a racing driver to have all vital controls at his fingertips. Instruments must be visible at a glance and meaningfully marked. Seats must be supple yet firm and supporting to provide complete comfort during long hours at high speed. The buyer of a Jaguar knows, in his first moments behind the wheel, that all these points and more have been mastered.

Inset into the reflection-proof matt black leather panel are the classic circular instruments, the sensory system of the agile XK-E. Prominent are the speedometer, with trip indicator, and the tachometer. Other instruments include the battery condition indicator, fuel gauge, transistorized electric clock and gauges of water temperature and oil pressure. Warning lights signal bright headlights and low fluid levels in the fuel tank and brake master cylinder. Below the instruments are the ten flush-fitting rocker-type switches that control the Jaguar's vital functions.

Other cockpit features show the XK-E's racing heritage. The alloy-spoked wood-rimmed steering wheel has a telescopically adjustable column. The hand brake is of fly-off type for quick starts. The short, stiff gear lever has a new oil-proof sheath. The extravagantly comfortable bucket seats are trimmed in selected prime hides. New in 1969 are the adjustable head rests and the new regulators for the reclining seat backs. Optional on the XK-E Roadster, Coupe and 2 + 2 are items of equipment which those who raced Jaguars were not permitted to enjoy: a radio, and an air conditioning plant.

The Coventry designers have subtly reshaped the XK-E lighting array to improve illumination and identification, meeting the latest safety regulations. Headlights are moved slightly forward within their chrome-rimmed coves. Side marker lights are provided at front and rear. Rear light units, incorporating the the back-up lights, are recessed beneath the rear bumper. A neat new chrome-plated frame encloses the license plate area. These refinements mark the first important change in appearance for the classic XK-E.

In North America there are certain features that are indispensable on a sports-luxury car: automatic transmission, air conditioning, power steering and power-boosted disc brakes at all four wheels, with lavish comfort for two and occasional seating for two more. Such are the accoutrements of the latest 2 + 2 version of the XK-E, with some of its popular options. Also optional on this unique grand tourer are whitewall tires, tinted glass and an electrically heated rear window defroster.

Jaguar's deceptively sleek four-seater is even cleaner in profile this year with a more steeply raked windshield. Nine inches longer in wheelbase than the other XK-E's, the 2 + 2 Coupe has a fully upholstered rear seat which can also be folded ingeniously forward to extend the luggage platform.

Incomparably equipped for its price, the 2 ¦ 2 Coupe is entirely updated this year with high, stronger bumpers and a larger front air inlet. Running and signal lights are enlarged for added safety, and more fully protected from minor damage. Other identification points of the new model include the more forward headlamp placement and the adjustable headrests on the genuine leather front bucket seats.

No other car is capable of offering faster or safer transportation for you and your family.

Main dimensions: Wheelbase 105 ins. Track 50 ins. front and rear. Overall length 184¼ ins. Overall width 65¼ ins. Overall height 50 ins. Ground clearance (laden) 5½ ins. Turns lock to lock 2½. Turning circle 41 ft. Fuel capacity 16¾ gal. Oil capacity 9 qts. Water system 19¼ qts. Dry weight 2,744 lbs. Wheels and tires 15-inch wire-spoke, quick-change hub caps. Dunlop "Aquajet" radial ply 185 x 15 tires and tubes.

Body features: Same as Coupe with the addition of a fully upholstered rear seat for two. The back of the rear seat is horizontally split, permitting the upper half to move forward to increase luggage space to maximum length of 52½ ins. Reclining seats with adjustable headrests. Variable-direction ventilation nozzles on panel.

Optional equipment: Fully automatic transmission with dual-drive range and floor selector. Power steering. Chromium plated wire wheels. Whitewall tires. Tinted glass. Electrically heated rear window. Factory air conditioning.

Chassis features: Six-cylinder twin-overhead-camshaft XK engine. Bore and stroke 3.63 x 4.17 ins. Displacement 4235 cc; 258.4 cu. ins. Compression ratio 9 to 1 with hemispherical combustion chambers. 246 bhp at 5500 rpm; 263 lbs.-ft. of torque at 3000 rpm. Twin Zenith-Stromberg carburetors. Duplex air pollution control manifold. Dual exhaust systems. Oil coil ignition. 12-volt electrical system with heavy duty alternator. Hydraulically-operated clutch. Four-speed transmission, fully synchronized, floor shift. Limited slip differential. Stressed-skin all-steel monocoque body, with front and rear attached suspension and engine sub-frames. Independent front suspension by parallel wishbones, with torsion bars, telescopic shock absorbers and anti-roll bar. Independent rear suspension comprises transverse links, radius arms, quadruple coil springs with four concentric shock absorbers. Rack and pinion steering. Girling four-wheel power-assisted disc brakes.

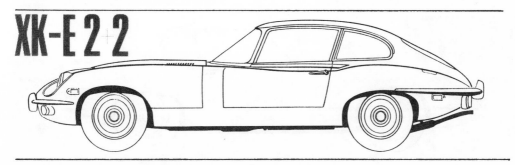

XK-E 2+2

The Jaguar XK-E Roadster is a beautiful two-seater sports car. It is also much more than that. It is five great victories at Le Mans. It is country living in the city. It is Briggs Cunningham, Walt Hansgen and Alfred Momo. It is the sparkle of 72-spoke chromed wire wheels spinning down Wilshire Boulevard. And it is a speedometer that reads to 160 mph because it has to.

Some XK-E Roadster features are classic, unchangeable. Such is the svelte, wind-formed shape, with the louvered hood hinging upward for total access to the aluminum-head twin-camshaft engine, tamed from racing for your enjoyment on the road. And there could be no replacement for the form-fitting reclining seats, the short, stiff lever between them that controls a fully-synchronized four-speed transmission (over 100 miles an hour in third).

Selective improvements in the latest XK-E Roadsters will be applauded by the urbanite: High, bolder bumpers both front and rear, better protection for bright signal lights and wide-spaced exhaust pipes, and a larger front air inlet (an XK-E has no "grille") for maximum cooling when the optional air conditioning is operating in traffic.

Have you ever owned an air-conditioned Jaguar Roadster? Why not this year?

Main dimensions: Wheelbase 96 ins. Track 50 ins. front and rear. Overall length 175-5/16 ins. Overall width 65¼ ins. Overall height 48 ins. Ground clearance (laden) 5½ ins. Turns lock to lock 2¾. Turning circle 37 ft. Fuel capacity 16¾ gal. Oil capacity 9 qts. Water system 19¼ qts. Dry weight 2,464 lbs. Wheels and tires 15-inch wire-spoke, quick-change hub caps. Dunlop "Aquajet" Radial ply 185 x 15 tires and tubes.

Body features: Quick folding top, fully lined, mounted on a special frame to permit easy raising or lowering. Large rear window. Top concealed when lowered beneath waterproof cover. Access to the luggage compartment in the rear is by an internal key locking release, which raises the deck lid. Additional space for packages is provided behind the reclining seats with adjustable headrests. Lockable glove compartment.

Optional equipment: Lightweight hardtop. Chromium plated wire wheels. Whitewall tires. Tinted glass. Factory air conditioning.

Chassis features: Six-cylinder twin-overhead-camshaft XK engine. Bore and stroke 3.63 x 4.17 ins. Displacement 4,235 cc; 258.4 cu. ins. Compression ratio 9 to 1 with hemispherical combustion chambers. 246 bhp at 5500 rpm; 263 lbs.-ft. of torque at 3000 rpm. Twin Zenith-Stromberg carburetors. Duplex air pollution control manifold. Dual exhaust system. Oil coil ignition. 12-volt electrical system with heavy duty alternator. Hydraulically-operated clutch. Four-speed transmission, fully synchronized, floor shift. Limited slip differential. Stressed-skin all-steel monocoque body, with front and rear attached suspension and engine sub-frames. Independent front suspension by parallel wishbones, with torsion bars, telescopic shock absorbers and anti-roll bar. Independent rear suspension comprises transverse links, radius arms, quadruple coil springs with four concentric shock absorbers. Rack and pinion steering. Girling four-wheel power-assisted disc brakes.

ROADSTER

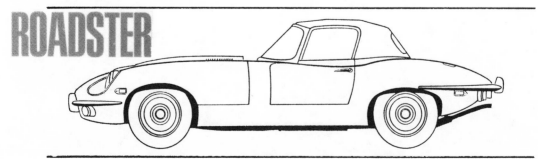

Does anyone really need a Jaguar XK-E Coupe? Is there any compelling necessity to own the equivalent of a Gemini capsule for the highway? Many people find they are able to resist the appeal of triple windshield wipers, of a real wood-rimmed aluminum-spoke adjustable steering wheel, of an independent suspension system so supple and precise that the XK-E Coupe becomes an uncanny extension of the driver's senses and desires.

If you cannot resist the XK-E Coupe you'll find it an immensely satisfying and practical automobile. Specially appropriate to this model are the adjustable headrests and new colors, Regency Red and Silver Gray, that are part of the complete XK-E range this year. Factory-fitted air conditioning, a highly-prized Coupe option, operates more efficiently with the larger front air intake of the new XK-E's.

New high, full-width bumpers protect the long nose and the tapered tail, with its wide door offering easy access to the roomy luggage platform. Handsome rocker-type switches, a padded cowl and recessed door handles add luxury while ensuring that the XK-E Coupe, like all Jaguars, meets and exceeds the Federal Safety Standards.

If this kind of personalized motoring appeals to you, you probably already own an XK-E Coupe. How about a new one?

Main dimensions: Wheelbase 96 ins. Track 50 ins. front and rear. Overall length 175-5/16 ins. Overall width 65¼ ins. Overall height 48 ins. Ground clearance (laden) 5½ ins. Turns lock to lock 2¾. Turning circle 37 ft. Fuel capacity 16¾ gal. Oil capacity 9 qts. Water system 19¼ qts. Dry weight 2,570 lbs. Wheels and tires 15-inch wire-spoke, quick-change hub caps. Dunlop "Aquajet" radial ply 185 x 15 tires and tubes.

Body features: Large window in rear luggage door, opened by internal release. Rear quarter windows hinged for ventilation. Luggage carried in flat, padded area behind seats, with hinged retainer at front that drops down to increase usable area. Reclining seats with adjustable headrests. Lockable glove compartment. Twin package shelves.

Optional equipment: Chromium plated wire wheels; whitewall tires; tinted glass; electrically heated rear window; factory air conditioning.

Chassis features: Six-cylinder twin-overhead-camshaft XK engine. Bore and stroke 3.63 x 4.17 ins. Displacement 4235 cc; 258.4 cu. ins. Compression ratio 9 to 1 with hemispherical combustion chambers. 246 bhp at 5500 rpm; 263 lbs.-ft of torque at 3000 rpm. Twin Zenith-Stromberg carburetors. Duplex air pollution control manifold. Dual exhaust system. Oil coil ignition. 12-volt electrical system with heavy duty alternator. Hydraulically-operated clutch. Four-speed transmission, fully synchronized, floor shift. Limited slip differential. Stressed-skin all-steel monocoque body, with front and rear attached suspension and engine sub-frames. Independent front suspension by parallel wishbones, with torsion bars, telescopic shock absorbers and anti-roll bar. Independent rear suspension comprises transverse links, radius arms, quadruple coil springs with four concentric shock absorbers. Rack and pinion steering. Girling four-wheel power-assisted disc brakes.

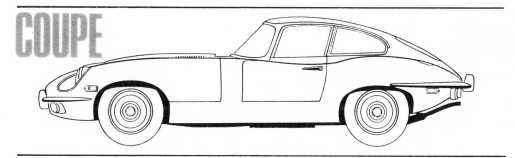

COUPE

83

JOD/PLAN

How To Place Your Order
All that is necessary is a visit to your nearest Jaguar dealer to select the exact model, and colors for the exterior and interior of the car. Make sure you buy through the American dealer to whom you will be going for future service. Payment is normally arranged with a small deposit and full payment 30 days before delivery.

Documentation has been reduced to a minimum. For Britain, car purchase order form and purchase tax exemption form (in duplicate). Both will be completed by the dealer. For the Continent, car purchase order form and Power of Attorney form (in duplicate), necessary to speed car registration in advance of arrival.

Take Delivery In Any Major City
Delivery charges vary according to the country and city chosen, and the distance from the Jaguar factory in Coventry, England. Charges range for example from Coventry itself ($39), London ($56), Paris ($182) to Rome ($346). These charges include delivery by bonded bi-lingual drivers; license plates; and associate membership in the Royal Automobile Club, which has representatives at all major ports and cities; and who offer many useful services for the motorist. Current American driver's license covers you in most countries.

Airport or dockside deliveries are not necessarily recommended due to the uncertainties of late or even early arrivals. But such deliveries can be arranged at an extra charge of $15 in the U.K. or $25 extra on the Continent.

Car insurance is compulsory abroad and can be arranged through the International Department of the American Automobile Association.

Arrangements For Shipping The Car Home
Return shipment is easily arranged and instructions can be confirmed before actually leaving the U.S.A., through the Jaguar shipping agents Dunnington and Arnold, Inc., 19 Rector Street, New York, N.Y. 10006; or abroad through the Jaguar factory representative or through a shipping agent. Shipping and marine insurance charges are for the account of the purchaser.

In Britain the car can be left with the Jaguar London shipping agents or at the factory itself in Coventry. It is then shipped to the U.S.A. with other new Jaguars under factory supervision. Cost varies according to model and ports, from about $250 from England to East Coast U.S.A.

Estimated Return Shipping Charges (including marine insurance)
(XJ Sedan and 2+2 long chassis Coupe charges slightly higher than Roadster and Coupe) U.S. East Coast ports $247/293 approx., U.S. Gulf ports $267/313, U.S. Great Lakes ports $252/281, U.S. West Coast ports $322/388.

Jaguar 1969 Models
(Overseas Delivery Tax-Free Prices to American Safety & Air Pollution Control Specifications.) Specifications and prices subject to change without notice. All orders subject to $6 cable charge.

Accessories Available
XK-E: Whitewall tires $22, Turbo disc wheels $58, Chrome wire wheels $107, Air-cond. $438, Tinted glass (roadster) $22, (coupe and 2 + 2) $31, Electrically-heated rear window (coupe and 2 + 2) $41, Detachable hard top (roadster) $172, Power steering (2 + 2) $138. **XJ Luxury Sedan:** Whitewall tires $37, Air-cond. $489, Tinted glass $73, Electrically-heated rear window $38, Electrically-operated windows $109. **All Models:** AM/FM Radio, Manual antenna $121, Power antenna $158.

Item	Overseas Delivery (Ex-Works)	U.S. Retail Suggested Price (P.O.E.)[i]	Difference
Roadster	$4,183	$5,534	$1,351
Coupe	$4,337	$5,725	$1,388
2+2 Coupe	$4,467	$5,907	$1,440
2+2 Coupe*	$4,661	$6,145	$1,484
XJ Sedan *	$4,723	$6,270	$1,547
XJ Sedan +	$4,881	$6,465	$1,584
Automatic *	Overdrive +	East Coast [i]	

United Kingdom Delivery Charges
Coventry $39	Liverpool $58	Glasgow $85
London $56	Southampton $67	Edinburgh $85

Continental Delivery Charges
Algeciras $366	Geneva $259	Oslo $368
Amsterdam $194	Genoa $329	Ostend $165
Basle $245	Gibraltar $366	Paris $182
Barcelona $320	Le Havre $201	Rotterdam $194
Brussels $165	Lausanne $264	Rome $346
Cannes $271	Lisbon $349	Salzburg $269
Cologne $249	Marseilles $271	Stockholm $344
Copenhagen $286	Munich $247	Venice $307
Cherbourg $201	Milan $305	Vienna $274
Dusseldorf $228	Madrid $341	Zurich $249
Frankfurt $240	Naples $366	
Florence $310	Nice $271	

ROADSTER

COUPE

2+2 COUPE
(optional automatic)

The chic, eclectic American woman trusts her own judgment. With a sure, infallible instinct for the best, she picks Wragge clothes and Jaguar sports cars, symbols of sleek motoring power from England. In 1969, she will choose the new 2+2 coupe, with automatic controls, power steering and a fully upholstered rear seat for extra passengers. Or the great new XKE roadster, with a cockpit full of sophisticated instruments.

the american woman collects wragge and jaguars

And of course she drives her new Jaguar with the Wragge clothes to complement. Greatcheck wool coat, *top left*, with patent belt. Textured cotton, *below left*, midriff turnout, belted with yellow silk Wragge signature scarf. Smashing white Moygashel linen pantsuit, *large figure*, with navy and red signature scarf. White linen dress, *below*, with red Wragge sunspots.

B. H. Wragge clothes for riding in Jaguars, at these stores: Hutzler's, Baltimore; H. & S. Pogue, Cincinnati; Boston Store, Milwaukee; Harold's, Minneapolis; Stix, Baer & Fuller, St. Louis; Gus Mayer, all stores; Swanson's, Kansas City; Iverson's, Tulsa; Frost Bros., San Antonio; Neusteters, Denver.

JAGUAR XK-E XJ SEDAN

XK-E 1970

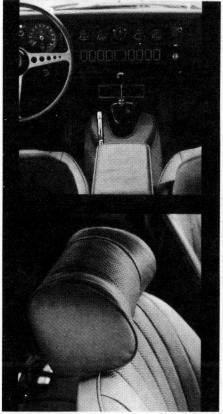

The exceptional breeding provided by a competition background is evident in all aspects of the XK-E, and most dramatically in the layout of the cockpit. It is essential for a racing driver to have all vital controls at his fingertips. Instruments must be visible at a glance and meaningfully marked. Seats must be supple yet firm and supporting to provide complete comfort during long hours at high speed. The buyer of a Jaguar knows, in his first moments behind the wheel, that all these points and more have been mastered.

Inset into the reflection-proof matt black leather panel are the classic circular instruments, the sensory system of the agile XK-E. Prominent are the speedometer, with trip indicator, and the tachometer. Other instruments include the battery condition indicator, fuel gauge, transistorized electric clock and gauges of water temperature and oil pressure. Warning lights signal bright headlights and low fluid levels in the fuel tank and brake master cylinder. Below the instruments are the ten flush-fitting rocker-type switches that control the Jaguar's vital functions; and at either side illuminated choke and heater controls.

Other cockpit features show the XK-E's racing heritage. The alloy-spoked wood-rimmed steering wheel has a telescopically adjustable column. The hand brake is of fly-off type for quick starts. The short, stiff gear lever has an oil-proof sheath. The extravagantly comfortable ventilated bucket seats are trimmed in selected prime hides, now with new type adjustable head rests and new regulators for the reclining seat backs. Optional on the XK-E Roadster, Coupe and 2 + 2 are items of equipment which those who raced Jaguars were not permitted to enjoy: a radio, and an air conditioning plant.

The Coventry designers have subtly reshaped the XK-E lighting array to improve illumination and identification, meeting the latest safety regulations. Headlights are moved slightly forward within their chrome-rimmed coves. Side marker lights are provided at front and rear. Rear light units, incorporating the back-up lights, are recessed beneath the rear bumper. A neat new chrome-plated frame encloses the license plate area. These refinements mark the first important change in appearance for the classic XK-E.

The Jaguar XK-E Roadster is a beautiful two-seater sports car. It is also much more than that. It is five great victories at Le Mans. It is country living in the city. It is Briggs Cunningham, Walt Hansgen and Alfred Momo. It is the sparkle of 72-spoke chromed wire wheels spinning down Wilshire Boulevard. And it is a speedometer that reads to 160 mph because it has to.

Some XK-E Roadster features are classic, unchangeable. Such is the svelte, wind-formed shape, with the louvered hood hinging upward for total access to the aluminum-head twin-camshaft engine, tamed from racing for your enjoyment on the road. And there could be no replacement for the form-fitting reclining seats, the short, stiff lever between them that controls a fully-synchronized four-speed transmission.

Selective improvements in the latest XK-E Roadsters will be applauded by the urbanite: High, bolder bumpers both front and rear, better protection for bright signal lights and wide-spaced exhaust pipes, and a larger front air inlet (an XK-E has no "grille") for maximum cooling when the optional air conditioning is operating in traffic.

Have you ever owned an air-conditioned Jaguar Roadster? Why not this year?

Main dimensions: Wheelbase 96 ins. Track 50 ins. front and rear. Overall length 175-5/16 ins. Overall width 65¼ ins. Overall height 48 ins. Ground clearance (laden) 5½ ins. Turns lock to lock 2¾. Turning circle 37 ft. Fuel capacity 16¾ gal. Oil capacity 9 qts. Water system 19¼ qts. Dry weight 2,464 lbs. Wheels and tires 15-inch wire-spoke, quick-change hub caps. Dunlop "Aquajet" radial ply 185 x 15 tires.

Body features: Quick folding top, fully lined, mounted on a special frame to permit easy raising or lowering. Large rear window. Top concealed when lowered beneath waterproof cover. Access to the luggage compartment in the rear is by an internal locking release, which raises the deck lid. Additional space for packages is provided behind the reclining seats with adjustable head rests. Lockable glove compartment.

Optional equipment: Lightweight hardtop. Power-assisted steering. Chromium plated wire wheels. Whitewall tires. Tinted glass. Factory air conditioning. Radio.

Chassis features: Six-cylinder twin-overhead-camshaft XK engine. Bore and stroke 3.63 x 4.17 ins. Displacement 4,235 cc; 258.4 cu. ins. Compression ratio 9 to 1 with hemispherical combustion chambers. 245 bhp at 5500 rpm; 263 lbs.-ft. of torque at 3000 rpm. Twin Zenith-Stromberg carburetors. Air pollution control manifold. Dual exhaust system. Oil coil ignition. 12-volt electrical system with heavy-duty alternator. Ignition warning buzzer. Back-up lights standard. Hydraulically-operated clutch. Four-speed transmission, fully synchronized, floor shift. Limited slip differential. Ratio 3.54 to 1. Stressed-skin all-steel monocoque body, with front and rear attached suspension and engine sub-frames. Independent front suspension by parallel wishbones, with torsion bars, telescopic shock absorbers and anti-roll bar. Independent rear suspension comprises transverse links, radius arms, quadruple coil springs with four concentric shock absorbers. Rack and pinion steering with adjustable steering wheel. Steering lock. Girling four-wheel power-assisted disc brakes.

ROADSTER

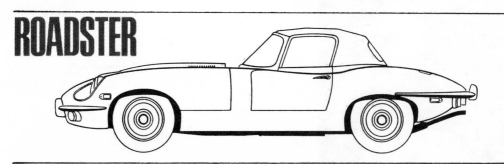

Does anyone really need a Jaguar XK-E Coupe? Is there any compelling necessity to own the equivalent of a Gemini capsule for the highway? Many people find they are able to resist the appeal of triple windshield wipers, of a real wood-rimmed aluminum-spoke adjustable steering wheel, of an independent suspension system so supple and precise that the XK-E Coupe becomes an uncanny extension of the driver's senses and desires.

If you cannot resist the XK-E Coupe you'll find it an immensely satisfying and practical automobile. Specially appropriate to this model are the new adjustable headrests and traditional color British Racing Green that are also part of the complete XK-E range. Factory-fitted air conditioning, a highly-prized Coupe option, operates more efficiently with the larger front air intake of the new XK-E's.

New high, full-width bumpers protect the long nose and the tapered tail, with its wide third door offering easy access to the roomy luggage platform. Handsome rocker-type switches, a padded cowl and recessed door handles add luxury while ensuring that the XK-E Coupe, like all Jaguars, meets and exceeds the Federal Safety Standards.

If this kind of personalized motoring appeals to you, you probably already own an XK-E Coupe. How about a new one?

Main dimensions: Wheelbase 96 ins. Track 50 ins. front and rear. Overall length 175-5/16 ins. Overall width 65¼ ins. Overall height 48 ins. Ground clearance (laden) 5½ ins. Turns lock to lock 2¾. Turning circle 37 ft. Fuel capacity 16¾ gal. Oil capacity 9 qts. Water system 19¼ qts. Dry weight 2,570 lbs. Wheels and tires 15-inch wire-spoke, quick-change hub caps. Dunlop ''Aquajet'' radial ply 185 x 15 tires.

Body features: Large window in rear luggage door, opened by internal release. Rear quarter windows hinged for ventilation. Luggage carried in flat, padded area behind seats, with hinged retainer at front that drops down to increase usable area. Reclining seats with adjustable head rests. Lockable glove compartment. Twin package shelves.

Optional equipment: Power-assisted steering. Chromium plated wire wheels; whitewall tires; tinted glass; electrically heated rear window; factory air conditioning. Radio.

Chassis features: Six-cylinder twin-overhead-camshaft XK engine. Bore and stroke 3.63 x 4.17 ins. Displacement 4235 cc; 258.4 cu. ins. Compression ratio 9 to 1 with hemispherical combustion chambers. 245 bhp at 5500 rpm; 263 lbs.-ft. of torque at 3000 rpm. Twin Zenith-Stromberg carburetors. Air pollution control manifold. Dual exhaust system. Oil coil ignition. 12-volt electrical system with heavy-duty alternator. Ignition warning buzzer. Back-up lights standard. Hydraulically-operated clutch. Four-speed transmission, fully synchronized, floor shift. Limited slip differential. Ratio 3.54 to1. Stressed-skin all-steel monocoque body, with front and rear attached suspension and engine sub-frames. Independent front suspension by parallel wishbones, with torsion bars, telescopic shock absorbers and anti-roll bar. Independent rear suspension comprises transverse links, radius arms, quadruple coil springs with four concentric shock absorbers. Rack and pinion steering with adjustable steering wheel. Steering lock. Girling four-wheel power-assisted disc brakes.

COUPE

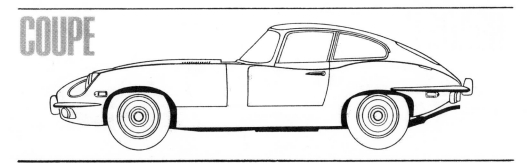

In North America there are certain features that are indispensable in a sports-luxury car: automatic transmission, air conditioning, power steering and power-boosted disc brakes at all four wheels, with lavish comfort for two and occasional seating for two more. Such are the accoutrements of the latest 2 + 2 version of the XK-E, with some of its popular options. Also optional on this unique grand tourer are whitewall tires, tinted glass, and an electrically heated rear window defroster.

Jaguar's deceptively sleek four-seater is now even cleaner in profile with a more steeply raked windshield. Nine inches longer in wheelbase than the other XK-E's, the 2 + 2 Coupe has a fully upholstered rear seat which can also be folded ingeniously forward to extend the luggage platform.

Incomparably equipped for its price, the latest 2 + 2 Coupe has high, stronger bumpers and a larger front air inlet. Running and signal lights are enlarged for added safety, and more fully protected from minor damage. Other identification points of the new model include the more forward headlamp placement and the adjustable headrests on the genuine leather ventilated bucket seats.

No other car is capable of offering faster or safer transportation for you and family.

Main dimensions: Wheelbase 105 ins. Track 50 ins. front and rear. Overall length 184¼ ins. Overall width 65¼ ins. Overall height 50 ins. Ground clearance (laden) 5½ ins. Turns lock to lock 2½. Turning circle 41 ft. Fuel capacity 16¾ gal. Oil capacity 9 qts. Water system 19¼ qts. Dry weight 2,744 lbs. Wheels and tires 15-inch wire-spoke, quick-change hub caps. Dunlop "Aquajet" radial ply 185 x 15 tires.

Body features: Same as Coupe with the addition of a fully upholstered rear seat for two. The back of the rear seat is horizontally split, permitting the upper half to move forward to increase luggage space to maximum length of 52½ ins. Reclining seats with adjustable headrests. Variable-direction ventilation nozzles on panel.

Optional equipment: Fully automatic transmission with dual-drive range and floor selector. Ratio 3.31 to 1. Power-assisted steering. Chromium plated wire wheels. Turbo-disc wheels. Whitewall tires. Tinted glass. Electrically heated rear window. Factory air conditioning. Radio.

Chassis features: Six-cylinder twin-overhead-camshaft XK engine. Bore and stroke 3.63 x 4.17 ins. Displacement 4235 cc; 258.4 cu. ins. Compression ratio 9 to 1 with hemispherical combustion chambers 245 bhp at 5500 rpm; 263 lbs.-ft. of torque at 3000 rpm. Twin Zenith-Stromberg carburetors. Air pollution control manifold. Dual exhaust systems. Oil coil ignition. 12-volt electrical system with heavy-duty alternator. Ignition warning buzzer. Back-up lights standard. Hydraulically-operated clutch. Four-speed transmission, fully synchronized, floor shift. Limited slip differential. Ratio 3.54 to 1. Stressed-skin all-steel monocoque body, with front and rear attached suspension and engine sub-frames. Independent front suspension by parallel wishbones, with torsion bars, telescopic shock absorbers and anti-roll bar. Independent rear suspension comprises transverse links, radius arms, quadruple coil springs with four concentric shock absorbers. Rack and pinion steering with adjustable steering wheel, steering lock. Girling four-wheel power-assisted disc brakes.

XK-E 2 2

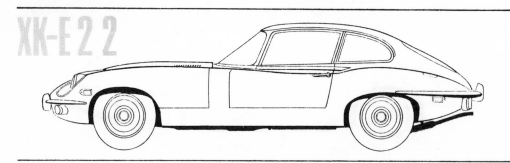

There's a special feeling people have about Jaguar. It's a feeling that becomes evident in a number of ways. Some people just look at the car and breathe deeply, others run their hands along the fenders, caress the leather seats or play with the steering wheel.

The feeling that is strongest is the feeling the Jaguar owner has for his own different breed of cat; the comfortable partnership feeling between man and machine. He likes to drive down a straightaway and make the miles disappear. He likes to ease into a corner and delicately dance through the turns in complete control. He likes the feel of the butter-soft leather and he likes the way the seat holds him. He likes the way people look at him.

There is nothing in the world to compare with the Jaguar feeling and there's only one way to get it. Buy one.

XK-E. A powerful 4.2 litre double overhead camshaft engine responsive at all speeds, effortless shifting with the 4-speed fully synchromesh gearbox and diaphragm clutch. Big, safe stopping power from any speed with 4-wheel, power-assisted disc brakes and an extra margin of safety with 2 independent hydraulic braking systems, front and rear. Add quick, accurate rack-and-pinion steering and independent suspension that keeps all 4 wheels on the ground even on the roughest roads. This is the Jaguar XK-E, a sleek aerodynamic dart of lightweight all-steel monocoque construction, fitted with bucket seats upholstered in finest leather and worked to painstaking excellence throughout.

3.8 'S'. The 4-door family sedan that looks and acts like a sports car. A special XK 3.8 litre engine throbs with power and a 4-speed gearbox with overdrive or Borg-Warner automatic transmission (your choice) makes it move; 4-wheel, power-assisted disc brakes stop it, safe and sure every time, time after time. The all-around independent suspension lets you know you are in a car, but gently. On the inside, matched walnut paneling, English glove leather and thick wool pile announce the distinctive luxury attained by men who care about making great motorcars.

4.2 Sedan. Someplace, sometime, every man who cares about fine luxury motorcars should experience the inimitable pleasure of driving the Jaguar 4.2 Sedan. Powered by the famous 4.2 litre XK engine, acceleration is eye-opening and variable ratio power steering makes handling this car as sure, as exhilarating an experience as guiding an XK-E through the turns. Power-assisted, 4-wheel disc brakes stop the sedan quickly, safely, effortlessly and all-around independent suspension gives you a ride that is controlled for maximum comfort. When you sit behind the wheel and look at the neat array of dials and switches on the polished walnut dash, feel the deep richness of the fine grain leather upholstery and smell the luxury of newness, you will come face-to-face with an unalterable fact: the Jaguar 4.2 Sedan is one of the finest motorcars in the world.

If you're going to Europe, money-saving overseas delivery can be easily arranged. See your nearest dealer, or write Jaguar Cars Inc., 32 East 57th Street, New York, N.Y. 10022.

Jaguar: A different breed of cat.

5.2 Liter Series III

During the sixties Jaguar built a mid-engine prototype LeMans style road racer, the XJ-13. Just as the D-Type had pointed the way toward the original XK-E, this XJ-13 previewed future Jaguar sports cars. The XJ-13 featured a four cam (two per head) V-12 engine. This led to speculation that a twelve cylinder powerplant was in the works. The venerable XK six cylinder engine had been around since the late-forties and it was getting a little long in the tooth.

Thus it was not a total surprise when Jaguar announced the all-aluminum V-12 engine early in 1971. Unlike the earlier XJ-13 engine, the production version featured only one cam per head. Earlier experiments with the twin cam engines showed them to be too bulky and too costly for the slightly extra power they provided at top end. Although the V-12 was 80 pounds heavier than the old six cylinder engine and still carried all the required smog equipment, performance was back in the same ball park as early XK-Es. The gasoline consumption penalty for the V-12 was only about three miles per gallon. The inherent smoothness of a twelve cylinder motor was another benefit.

There was definite status value associated with the V-12 engine. Only Ferrari and Lamborghini were building twelve cylinder engines at the time of Jaguar's introduction. They wanted twice as much for theirs due to their extremely low volume. Other exotic marques were offering nothing more than V-8s. In fact, it had not been since the late-forties that a manufacturer (Lincoln) had offered a twelve cylinder car in any kind of volume production.

During 1971, the XK-E was the only Jaguar to offer the V-12 engine. Although originally designed for the XJ sedan, it was not used there until July, 1972. This new engine heralded a Series III 5.3 Liter XK-E. Other changes were made to the E-Type along with the new engine. The two-passenger coupe was discontinued leaving only the 2+2 coupe and the roadster. The latter used the extended wheelbase of the 2+2. This allowed the availability of the automatic transmission in the roadster, as it had been fairly popular in the 2+2 and permitted increased storage capacity. The roadster did not feature the cramped jump seats of the coupe. Wider tires were used on both models. The track was increased 3 1/4" in front and 4 1/4" in the rear. Wire wheels, which had been standard equipment, became an extra-cost option. Many XK-Es were now seen with the sedan-style chromed steel wheels. There was a new eggcrate grille with two bumperettes to replace the full width bumper up front. A V-12 emblem was added to the rear. Inside, a smaller, black leather rimmed wheel replaced the wood steering wheel of previous models. In March, 1972, a new, larger fiberglass top was offered for the roadster. The ventilation system was improved with fresh-air vents in the cockpit. North America bound cars were fitted with remote control door mirrors and a seat belt alarm. In 1974, cars destined for the United States were fitted with a pair of large rubber bumper guards in the front and rear. These were necessary to meet the U.S. government crash test requirements. Home market cars were not plagued with these unsightly appendages.

British Leyland's U.S. marketing arm sponsored two Series III V-12 roadsters in SCCA racing from 1974 to 1976. The east coast based car was prepared by Group 44, Inc. The west coast vehicle was fielded by Haffaker Engineering. In their initial 1974 season they won their class against stiff competition. To the delight of the British factory, these cars proved the inherent performance of the XK-E even at the end of her production.

During the early seventies, Jaguar was facing sales competition from new sources. Chevrolet was fielding the less costly Camaro in addition to its traditional competitor, Corvette. Plus, there was the Pontiac Firebird and the Datsun 240-Z. Each of these three were offering styling and performance close to the Jaguar's at a fraction of Jaguar's cost. It seemed the tables had turned on the cat from Coventry. The marketing strategy Jaguar used against Ferrari and Maserati in 1961 was being employed by Pontiac and Datsun against Jaguar in 1974.

Not only was the styling getting long in the tooth compared to the competition. The XK-E's basic design was beginning to show its age as well. The fuel tank was located in a relatively vulnerable position in the rear. With various governments, led by the United States, requiring stricter crash tests, there was the distinct possibility the car wouldn't pass them without major alterations. After thirteen years of production and waning sales, the capital outlay hardly seemed justified.

The Series III models were the last of the XK-Es. The coupe was phased out in the fall of 1974. The last roadster was built in February, 1975. Over 72,000 cars had been built since 1961. Except for one special order green car, the last fifty roadsters were painted black. Series III production totalled 15,287 over its four year run. This amounted to only about 3,800 cars per year. Clearly sales were waning. Of this total, 7,990 were roadsters and 7,297 were 2+2-style coupes. The 2+2 total includes a few six cylinder Series III models that were built. No six cylinder Series III roadsters were made.

In the fall of 1975 Jaguar introduced the XJ-S, based on the XJ sedan. It was a larger, more refined car than the E-Type. To many it was a sporty car, not a sports car. Jaguar no longer catalogued a two-passenger car or an open car. Jaguar's "sports car" took on a new character.

The Series III was featured in a large catalogue issued in Britain in two editions dated 3/71 (see pages 100-116) and 3/73. There was a similar folder dated 3/71. There was another Canadian color sheet, numbered BLC 81 (see pages 128-129). There were two 1971 U.S. brochures, a folder (see page 99) and a large catalogue (see pages 118-127), both dated 3/71. The final item was a large folder, dated 3/73 (see pages 130-141).

THE E-TYPE WITH A DIFFERENCE

Ever since its very first appearance, the Jaguar E-Type has been instantly identifiable, all over the world, by its distinctive and highly individual styling and has become one of Britain's most successful exports.

Now, in Series Three form, it enters a new and even more exciting phase of its career. With many important advancements in design, and with the new Jaguar V12 engine as the principal feature, it continues to be one of the world's most desirable cars.

Depuis qu'elle est apparue pour la toute première fois on a reconnu la Jaguar Type E dans le monde entier aux lignes hautement individuelles qui la distinguent des autres et dans le domaine des exportations britanniques elle a rencontré le plus grand succès.

Maintenant sous la forme de la Serie Trois, sa carrière entre dans une nouvelle phase encore plus passionnante. Dotée de nombreux perfectionnements importants et du nouveau moteur Jaguar V12 qui en est la principale particularité elle continue d'être l'une des voitures les plus desirees au monde.

Alla sua comparsa, la Jaguar 'E' Type è stata immediatamente identificata ovunque, per la distinzione e stile spiccatamente personali. Tali qualità le hanno conferito una posizione di avanguardia nelle esportazioni dalla Gran Bretagna.

Nella versione Serie 3 Essa si affaccia ad una fase vieppiù eccitante, per via dei moglioramenti progettativi e del nuovo motore Jaguar V12, una delle caratteristiche più salienti, che ne fa la macchina oggigiorno più ambita.

Die hervorragende Linienführung des Jaguar E-Typ erkennt man sofort auf allen Strassen der Welt. Noch bestechender wirkt die neueste Version dieses begehrtesten Exportartikels Englands.

Das neueste, als Serie 3 bekannte Modell bietet seinen Enthusiasten noch mehr. Zahlreiche fortschrittliche Neuerungen, mit dem neuen V12-Motor an der Spitze, bahnen neue Wege der ständigen Weiterentwicklung im Automobilbau.

LA TYPE 'E' QUI EST DIFFÉRENTE
LA 'E' TYPE CHE SI DISTINGUE
DER E-TYPE MIT EINER DIFFERENZ

New features of the Series 5 E-Type

* A new JAGUAR ENGINE — the 5.3 litre V12 to supplement the 4.2 litre six cylinder 'XK' engine.

* A new version of the ROADSTER — with the 2+2 coupé wheelbase. Longer, roomier and with increased luggage space.

* ANTI-DIVE front suspension geometry — provides improved roadholding, particularly under braking.

* WIDER TRACK — for even higher standard of roadholding and cornering.

* DISC BRAKES — improved cooling by use of ventilated discs at the front and air scoops at the rear to match the performance of the car.

* STEERING — rack and pinion with power assistance standard. All models have new dished steering wheel with leather covered rim; collapsible upper and lower columns for safety; new rack mounting for even better response.

* HEATING AND DEMISTING — improved, high capacity system. Through-flow ventilation on 2+2 and hardtop models.

* TURNING CIRCLE — improved to 36 ft.

* FUEL TANK — increased to 18 gallons capacity.

* AUTOMATIC TRANSMISSION — now offered on roadster as well as 2+2 coupé.

PLUS A LARGE NUMBER OF PRIMARY AND SECONDARY SAFETY FEATURES

NOUVELLES PARTICULARITÉS DE LA TYPE E SERIE 3

Un nouveau **MOTEUR JAGUAR** — le moteur V12 de 5,3 litres qui vient s'ajouter au moteur 'XK' de 4,2 litres a six cylindres • Une nouvelle variante de la **ROUTIERE** — avec empattement de coupé 2+2 Plus longue, avec plus d'espace et un plus grand coffre a bagages • Géométrie 'anti-piquage' de la suspension avant — permettant une meilleure tenue de la route, particulièrement lors du freinage • **VOIE PLUS LARGE** — on peut tenir la route et prendre les virages encore mieux • **FREINS A DISQUE** — leur refroidissement est amélioré grâce à des disques ajourés à l'avant et à des goulottes d'aération à l'arrière, pour répondre aux performances de la voiture • **DIRECTION** — à crémaillère et assistée, standard sur tous les modèles. Tous les modèles ont un nouveau volant concave avec jante garnie de cuir, colonnes supérieure et inférieure télescopiques, pour plus de sécurité, support de crémaillère de nouveau type qui permet à la direction de réagir encore mieux • **CHAUFFAGE ET DESEMBUAGE** — système perfectionné et a grand rendement. Ventilation "through-flow" sur les modèles 2+2 et hardtop • **RAYON DE BRAQUAGE** — maintenant de 5,5 mètres • **RÉSERVOIR D'ESSENCE** — maintenant de 82 litres • **TRANSMISSION AUTOMATIQUE** — possible maintenant sur la routière aussi bien que sur le coupé 2+2

ET AUSSI UN GRAND NOMBRE DE PARTICULARITÉS IMPORTANTES ET SECONDAIRES CONTRIBUANT A LA SÉCURITÉ

NUOVE CARATTERISTICHE DELLA E TYPE SERIE 3

Un nuovo **MOTORE JAGUAR** V12 di 5300 cc offerto come alternativa al motore a sei cilindri XK di 4200 cc • Una nuova versione **ROADSTER** — con il passo della coupé 2 + 2 Più lunga, più spaziosa e vani portabagagli più grande • Sospensione anteriore A **PROVA DI IMPENNATA** — perfetta tenuta di strada, particolarmente quando si frena • **CARREGGIATA PIU AMPIA** — per un miglior comportamento su strada ed in curva • **FRENI A DISCO** — a raffreddamento intensificato promosso da apposite ventilazioni sui freni anteriori e da prese d'aria dinamiche, sui freni posteriori, per adeguamento alle prestazioni della macchina • **STERZO** — a cremagliera, servoassistito, per tutti i modelli. Volante concavo di nuovo disegno con corona foderata di pelle per tutti i modelli; i due snodi arretrano in caso d'urto. Supporto della cremagliera migliorato per una pronta risposta del veicolo • **RISCALDAMENTO E VENTILAZIONE** — assicurati da un sistema perfezionato, di grande capacità. Rinnovo continuo dell'aria sulle versioni 2 + 2 ed a tetto rigido • **DIAMETRO DI STERZATA** — di soli metri 5 • **SERBATOIO DEL CARBURANTE** — della capacità di litri 82 • **CAMBIO AUTOMATICO** — attualmente per le versioni Roadster e Coupé 2 + 2.

E MOLTEPLICI ALTRI ACCORGIMENTI CHE ACCENTUANO ULTERIORMENTE LA SICUREZZA

NEUERUNGEN IM E-TYPE SERIE 3

Der neue **V12-JAGUAR-MOTOR** mit 5,3 Liter. Der 4,2 Sechszylinder "XK" Motor ist weiter wahlweise erhältlich • Eine neue **ROADSTER-VERSION** — mit dem Radstand des 2+2 Coupé. Länger, geräumiger und mit mehr Kofferraum • Vorderachsaufhangung mit **ANTI-DIVE-EFFEKT** — bessere Strassenlage, besonders beim scharfen Bremsen • **BREITE SPUR** für noch bessere Strassenlage und Spurhaltung • **SCHEIBENBREMSEN** — verbesserte Kühlung durch Belüftung der Scheibenbremsen an den Vorderrädern und Kühlrippen an der Hinterradbremse verbessern die Bremswirkung entsprechend der enormen Leistung des Wagens • **LENKUNG** — Zahnstangenlenkung mit Servounterstützung bei allen Modellen serienmässig. Lederlenkrader an allen Modellen. Sicherheits-Lenksäule bietet Aufprallschutz. Präzises Ansprechen der Lenkung durch neue Anordnung der Zahnstange • **HEIZUNG UND ENTFROSTUNG** — noch weiter verbessert, höhere Heizleistung "Through-flow" — Belüftung beim 2+2 Coupé und Hardtop Modellen • **WENDEKREIS** — nur 11 m • **KRAFTSTOFFTANK** — Fassungsvermögen auf 82 Liter vergrössert • **AUTOMATISCHES GETRIEBE** — wird sowohl beim Roadster als auch beim 2+2 Coupé angeboten.

SOWIE WEITERE SICHERHEITS-MERKMALE

Jaguar V-12:
The ultimate cat

Jaguar V-12

For an E type with a difference, a
catalogue which is different. More a
picture album in fact. Intended to
portray the car's affinity with the true
nature of grand touring and the
enjoyment which this kind of motoring
provides.

A voiture aussi différente que la Type E
Catalogue différent.
Plutôt qu'un catalogue
Un bel album.
Vous découvrirez dans ses pages le
caractère véritable du "grand tour" et les
joies qu'on connaît au volant d'une
telle voiture.

Per una Jaguar E "diversa" anche il
catalogo è diverso. Piu che catalogo è
una collezione d'immagini e figure,
per meglio illustrare l'affinità di questa
vettura di gran classe allo spirito del
vero gran turismo, e i piaceri di questo
genere di guida.

Fur einen besonderen Type E ein
besonderer Katalog. Eigentlich mehr ein
Photoalbum, das Ihnen die
Verwandschaft des Wagens zum Gran
Turismo und die Freude am Fahren
darstellt.

The means of grand touring, Jaguar
fashion. The 2 + 2 model and the
roadster version of the E type with a
difference.

Le "grand tour" mais en Jaguar.
La 2 + 2 et la version roadster de la
voiture Type E la
voiture vraiment différente.

Per fare del gran turismo, stile Jaguar,
le versioni 2 + 2 e spider del famoso
modello E, oggi però "diverso".

Gran Turismo — das heisst Reisen mit
Jaguar im grossen Stil, mit dem
2 + 2 Modell oder der Roadster Version.

The 2 + 2, depicted here against typical contrasting backgrounds of the grand tour.

La 2 + 2 s'inscrit ici sur les arrière-plans combien divers caractéristiques du "grand tour."

Il coupé 2 + 2 nelle contrastanti scenografie dei grandi viaggi.

Der 2 + 2 vor dem kontrastreichen Hintergrund der "Grossen Reisen."

The roadster provides contrasts of its
own; an open two-seater and an optional
detachable hard top.

La roadster est elle-même une voiture
de contrastes; deux places découverte
et en option hard top amovible.

La spider dalla doppia personalità:
due posti scoperti oppure hard top
smontabile, a richiesta.

Der Roadster selbst bietet Ihnen zwei
Kontraste als offener Zweisitzer oder mit
abnehmbaren Hardtop.

Here the pictures tell the story of
comfort and space.
The rear seat backrest in the 2 + 2 is
designed to form an extended baggage
floor when only two people use
the car.

Des photos qui vous parlent de confort
ét d'espace.
Le dossier arrière de la 2 + 2 est concu
pour agrandir le plancher aux bagages
quand il n'y a que deux personnes
à bord de la voiture.

L'immagine rende alla perfezione il
comfort e l'abitabilità di questa vettura.
Nel coupé 2 + 2 lo schienale dei
posti dietro diventa un ampio pianale
per i bagagli viaggiando in due.

Etwas vom Komfort und Raumlichkeit.
Bei 2 Personen ist die Rücksitzlehne als
Verlangerung des Kofferraumes
verwendbar.

A force to be reckoned with in the
grand touring scene. For with the E type
with a difference comes a choice of
power units — the in-line 6 or the V12.
Technical details are contained in
the back page of this catalogue.

Une force avec laquelle doivent compter
ceux qui font le "grand tour". Avec
la Type E, voiture différente, on a le choix
entre deux moteurs, 6 cylindres en
ligne ou 12 cylindres en V. Détails
techniques à la dernière page du
catalogue.

Gran Turismo dalle grandi potenze.
Per questa Jaguar E "diversa" c'è una
scelta di motori e potenze : 6 cilindri
in linea oppure 12 a V. L'esauriente
descrizione tecnica è riportata in
ultima pagina.

Eine Kraft, mit der man in der Gran
Turismo Klasse rechnen muss. Mit dem
Type E haben Sie die Wahl zwischene
dem 6 Zylinder und dem 12 Zylinder-
Motor.
Technische Einzelheiten finden Sie auf
der Rückseite dieses Kataloges.

Kaleidescope — aspects of the tour and of the Series Three E-Type.

Un kaléidoscope — quelques aspects du "grand tour" et de la Type E Série Trois.

Caleidoscopio — immagini del gran tour e della Jaguar E, Terza Serie.

Kaleidoskop — Schnappschüsse von der Reise mit dem Type E Serie 3.

THE E-TYPE WITH A DIFFERENCE

Ever since its very first appearance, the Jaguar E-Type has been instantly identifiable, all over the world, by its distinctive and highly individual styling and has become one of Britain's most successful exports.

Now, in Series Three form, it enters a new and even more exciting phase of its career. With many important advancements in design, and with the new Jaguar V12 engine as the principal feature, it continues to be one of the world's most desirable cars.

LA TYPE 'E' QUI EST DIFFÉRENTE

Depuis qu'elle est apparue pour la toute première fois on a reconnu la Jaguar Type E dans le monde entier aux lignes hautement individuelles qui la distinguent des autres et dans le domaine des exportations britanniques elle a rencontre le plus grand succès.

Maintenant sous la forme de la Série Trois, sa carrière entre dans une nouvelle phase encore plus passionnante. Dotée de nombreux perfectionnements importants et du nouveau moteur Jaguar V12 qui en est la principale particularité elle continue d'être l'une des voitures les plus désirées au monde.

LA 'E' TYPE CHE SI DISTINGUE

Alla sua comparsa, la Jaguar 'E' Type è stata immediatamente identificata ovunque, per la distinzione e stile spiccatamente personali. Tali qualità le hanno conferito una posizione di avanguardia nelle esportazioni dalla Gran Bretagna.

Nella versione Serie 3 Essa si affaccia ad una fase vieppiù eccitante, per via dei moglioramenti progettativi e del nuovo motore Jaguar V12, una delle caratteristiche più salienti, che ne fa la macchina oggigiorno più ambita.

DER E-TYPE MIT EINER DIFFERENZ

Die hervorragende Linienfuhrung des Jaguar E-Typ erkennt man sofort auf allen Strassen der Welt. Noch bestechender wirkt die neueste Version dieses begehrtesten Exportartikels Englands.

Das neueste, als Serie 3 bekannte Modell bietet seinen Enthusiasten noch mehr. Zahlreiche fortschrittliche Neuerungen, mit dem neuen V12-Motor an der Spitze, bahnen neue Wege der standigen Weiterentwicklung im Automobilbau.

NEW FEATURES OF THE SERIES 3 E-TYPE

* A new JAGUAR ENGINE — the 5.3 litre V12 to supplement the 4.2 litre six cylinder 'XK' engine.

* A new version of the ROADSTER — with the 2+2 coupé wheelbase. Longer, roomier and with increased luggage space.

* ANTI-DIVE front suspension geometry — provides improved roadholding, particularly under braking.

* WIDER TRACK — for even higher standard of roadholding and cornering.

* DISC BRAKES — improved cooling by use of ventilated discs at the front and air scoops at the rear to match the performance of the car.

* STEERING — rack and pinion with power assistance standard on all models. All models have new dished steering wheel with leather covered rim; collapsible upper and lower columns for safety; new rack mounting for even better response.

* HEATING AND DEMISTING — improved, high capacity system. Through-flow ventilation on 2+2 and hardtop models.

* TURNING CIRCLE — improved to 36 ft.

* FUEL TANK — increased to 18 gallons capacity.

* AUTOMATIC TRANSMISSION — now offered on roadster as well as 2+2 coupé.

PLUS A LARGE NUMBER OF PRIMARY AND SECONDARY SAFETY FEATURES

NOUVELLES PARTICULARITÉS DE LA TYPE E SERIÉ 3

Un nouveau **MOTEUR JAGUAR** le moteur V12 de 5,3 litres qui vient s'ajouter au moteur 'XK' de 4,2 litres à six cylindres ● Une nouvelle variante de la **ROUTIERE** avec empattement de coupé 2+2. Plus longue, avec plus d'espace et un plus grand coffre à bagages. ● Géométrie 'anti-piquage' de la suspension avant — permettant une meilleure tenue de la route, particulièrement lors du freinage ● **VOIE PLUS LARGE** — on peut tenir la route et prendre les virages encore mieux ● **FREINS A DISQUE** - leur refroidissement est amélioré grâce à des disques ajourés à l'avant et à des goulottes d'aération à l'arrière pour répondre aux performances de la voiture ● **DIRECTION** — à crémaillère et assistée, standard sur tous les modèles. Tous les modèles ont un nouveau volant concave avec jante garnie de cuir; colonnes supérieure et inférieure télescopiques pour plus de sécurité; support de crémaillère de nouveau type qui permet à la direction de réagir encore mieux ● **CHAUFFAGE ET DESEMBUAGE** — système perfectionné et à grand rendement. Ventilation ''through-flow'' sur les modèles 2+2 et hardtop ● **RAYON DE BRAQUAGE** maintenant de 5,5 mètres ● **RESERVOIR D'ESSENCE** maintenant de 82 litres ● **TRANSMISSION AUTOMATIQUE** possible maintenant sur la routière aussi bien que sur le coupé 2+2.

ET AUSSI UN GRAND NOMBRE DE PARTICULARITÉS IMPORT-ANTES ET SECONDAIRES CON-TRIBUANT À LA SÉCURITÉ.

NUOVE CARATTERISTICHE DELLA E TYPE SERIE 3

Un nuovo **MOTORE JAGUAR** V12 di 5300 cc. offerto come alternativa al motore a sei cilindri XK di 4200 cc ● Una nuova versione **ROADSTER** con il passo della coupé 2 + 2. Più lunga, più spaziosa e vano portabagagli più grande ● Suspensione anteriore **A PROVA DI IMPENNATA** — perfetta tenuta di strada, particolarmente quando si frena ● **CARREGGIATA PIU AMPIA** — per un miglior comportamento su strada ed in curva ● **FRENI A DISCO** – a raffreddamento intensificato promosso da apposite ventilazioni sui freni anteriori e da prese d'aria dinamiche, sui freni posteriori, per adeguamento alle prestazioni della macchina ● **STERZO** – a cremagliera, servoassistito, per tutti i modelli. Volante concavo di nuovo disegno con corona foderata di pelle per tutti i modelli; i due snodi arretrano in caso d'urto. Supporto della cremagliera migliorato per una pronta risposta del veicolo ● **RISCALDAMENTO E VENTILAZIONE** assicurati da un sistema perfezionato, di grande capacità. Rinnovo continuo dell'aria sulle versioni 2 + 2 ed a tetto rigido ● **DIAMETRO DI STERZATA** - di soli metri 11 ● **SERBATOIO DEL CARBURANTE** della capacità di litri 82 ● **CAMBIO AUTOMATICO** attualmente per le versioni Roadster e Coupé 2 + 2.

E MOLTEPLICI ALTRI ACCORGI-MENTI CHE ACCENTUANO ULTERIORMENTE LA SICUREZZA

NEUERUNGEN IM E-TYPE, SERIE 3

Der neue **V12-JAGUAR-MOTOR** mit 5,3 Liter. Der 4,2-Sechszylinder "XK" Motor ist weiter wahlweise erhältlich ● Eine neue **ROADSTER-VERSION** — mit dem Radstand des 2+2 Coupé. Länger, geräumiger und mit mehr Kofferaum ● Vorderachsaufhängung mit **ANTI-DIVE-EFFEKT** — bessere Strassenlage, besonders beim scharfen Bremsen ● **BREITE SPUR** — für noch bessere Strassenlage und Spurhaltung. ● **SCHEIBENBREMSEN** — verbesserte Kühlung durch Belüftung der Scheibenbremsen an den Vorderrädern und Kühlrippen an der Hinterradbremse verbessern die Bremswirkung entsprechend der enormen Leistung des Wagens ● **LENKUNG** — Zahnstangenlenkung mit Servounterstützung bei allen Modellen. Lederlenkräder an allen Modellen. Sicherheits-Lenksäule bietet Aufprallschutz. Präzises Ansprechen der Lenkung durch neue Anordnung der Zahnstange ● **HEIZUNG UND ENTFROSTUNG** — noch weiter verbessert, höhere Heizleistung. "Through-flow" — Belüftung beim 2+2 Coupe und Hardtop-Modellen ● **WENDEKREIS** — nur 11 m ● **KRAFTSTOFFTANK** — Fassungsvermögen auf 82 Liter vergrössert ● **AUTOMATISCHES GETRIEBE** — wird sowohl beim Roadster als auch beim 2+2 Coupé angeboten.

SOWIE WEITERE SICHERHEITS-MERKMALE

BRIEF SPECIFICATION

TRANSMISSION Choice of four-speed all-synchromesh manual gearbox or Borg Warner Model 12 automatic transmission (P,R,N,D,2,1).

SUSPENSION Fully independent suspension all round, incorporating anti-dive geometry at the front.

BRAKES Servo assisted disc brakes all round. Ventilated type at front. Dual fluid circuits for safety.

STEERING Rack and pinion type with power assistance. Collapsible upper and lower steering columns. Dished steering wheel with leather covered rim.

V12 ENGINE Twelve cylinder, 60° vee, 5.3 litre engine. 90mm bore x 70mm stroke. Capacity 5343 cc. Maximum bhp GROSS: 314 at 6200 rpm. DIN: 272 at 5850 rpm. Maximum torque GROSS: 349 lbs.ft. at 3800 rpm. DIN: 304 lb.ft. at 3600 rpm. Maximum BMEP GROSS: 151 psi at 3600 rpm. DIN: 141 psi at 3600 rpm. Compression ratio 9:1. Single overhead camshaft per bank. Four Zenith-Stromberg carburetters. Lucas Opus Mark 2 electronic ignition system. Vertical-flow radiator with thermostatically controlled electrical fans.

4.2 LITRE ENGINE In-line 6 cylinder, twin overhead camshaft, 'XK' engine with twin carburetters. Bore 92.07 mm. Stroke 106 mm. Capacity 4235 c.c. Max. BHP (Gross) 187 at 5,000 r.p.m. (DIN) 171 at 4,500 r.p.m. Max. Torque (Gross) 237 lbs.ft. at 3,000 r.p.m. (DIN) 230 lbs.ft. at 2,500 r.p.m.

WHEELS AND TYRES Wide rim painted, pressed-steel wheels with chromed rim embellishers. Dunlop SP Sport radial ply EV70VR15 tyres. Chrome plated pressed steel and chrome plated wire spoke wheels available as optional extras.

FUEL SUPPLY 18 gallon tank. Electric pump.

ELECTRICAL EQUIPMENT AND INSTRUMENTS Alternator. 12-volt battery. Negative earth system Pre-engaged starter motor. Lighting equipment includes hazard warning system. Instruments include oil pressure and water temperature gauges, and battery condition indicator. Twin, two-speed windscreen wipers. High velocity, twin-spray screen washer.

BODY Monocoque main section. Bolt-on subframe for engine and front suspension. Choice of open 2-seater (hardtop optional extra) and 2+2 fixed head coupe. Semi-reclining seats in both models.

HEATING AND DEMISTING High capacity fresh air heating and demisting system with through-flow ventilation on 2+2 and optional hard-top models.

PRINCIPAL DIMENSIONS Overall length 15ft. 4½ins. (468.4 cm). Overall width 5ft. 6 1/8ins. (167.8 cm). Wheelbase 8ft. 9ins. (266.7 cm). Track front 4ft. 6½ins. (138.7 cm). Track rear 4ft. 5ins. (134.6 cm). Turning circle 36ft. (11 m).

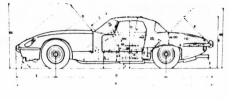
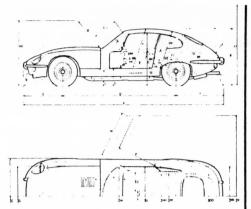
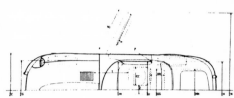

DIMENSIONS – FIXED HEAD COUPÉ

		Ins.	Cms.
A	Overall length	184.4	468.4
B	Overall height	51.4	130.6
C	Overall width	66.1	167.8
D	Wheelbase	105.0	266.7
E	Front overhang	36.3	92.0
F	Rear overhang	43.13	109.5
G	Front track	54.25	138.0
H	Rear track	53.25	135.3
J	Ground clearance – unladen	5.9	15.0
	– laden	5.4	13.7
K	Front clearance angle	21°	
L	Rear clearance angle	15°	
M	Door opening width	40.5	102.9
N	Overall width doors open	134.0	340.4
O	Ground to top of door	46.5	118.1
P	Door open aperture	35.0	88.9
Q	Bonnet aperture	33.7	85.7
R	Rear door aperture	28.0	71.1
S	Door step height	16.0	40.6
T	Windscreen depth	28.25	71.7
U	Shoulder room	49.0	124.5
V	Front headroom	35.5	90.2
W	Windscreen width (mean)	49.0	124.5
X	Pedals to cushion	19.75	50.2
Y	Front bulkhead to seat cushion	28.5	72.87
Z	Width between seats	9.0	22.9
AA	Front seat height	10.25	26.0
BB	Front seat depth	18.5	47.0
CC	Front seat width	17.8	45.3
DD	Rear headroom	33.0	83.8
EE	Rear seat height	10.0	25.4
FF	Rear seat depth	14.0	35.6
GG	Height of rear seat squab	17.0	43.2
HH	Width of rear seat squab (Min)	39.0	99.1
JJ	Steering wheel to cushion	8.6	21.9
KK	Steering wheel to seat squab	20	50.8
LL	Steering wheel reach adjustment	15	38.1
MM	Steering wheel diameter	2.75	5.7
NN	Rear knee room	7.5	19.1
OO	Maximum boot width	39.0	99.1
PP	Minimum boot width	36.0	91.4
QQ	Maximum boot length	52.5	133.4
RR	Minimum boot length	42.0	106.7
SS	Boot capacity	8-11 cu.ft.	0.22-0.31 cu.m.
TT	Maximum height boot open	72.5	184.1
UU	Maximum height bonnet open	58.3	148.0

DIMENSIONS – ROADSTER

		Ins.	Cms.
A	Overall length	184.4	468.4
B	Overall height	48.4	122.6
C	Overall width	66.1	167.8
D	Wheelbase	105.0	266.7
E	Front overhang	36.3	92.0
F	Rear overhang	43.1	109.5
G	Front track	54.25	138.0
H	Rear track	53.25	135.3
J	Ground clearance – unladen	5.9	15.0
	– laden	5.4	13.7
K	Front clearance angle	21°	
L	Rear clearance angle	15°	
M	Door opening width	40.5	102.9
N	Overall width doors open	134.0	310.4
O	Ground to top of door	43.0	109.2
P	Door open aperture	35.0	88.9
Q	Bonnet open aperture	33.7	85.7
R	Boot open aperture	29	73.7
S	Door step height	16	40.6
T	Windscreen depth	19.2	48.8
U	Shoulder room	49.5	125.8
V	Headroom	33.0	83.8
W	Windscreen width (mean)	50.0	127.0
X	Pedals to cushion	22.3	56.5
Y	Front bulkhead to seat cushion	31.8	82.0
Z	Width between seats	9.0	22.9
AA	Seat height	11.0	27.9
BB	Seat depth	18.5	47.0
CC	Seat width	17.8	45.3
DD	Seat back to rear bulkhead	15.8	40.0
EE	Rear parcel box height	21.5	31.8
FF	Maximum rear parcel box depth	8	20.3
GG	Rear parcel box length	38.3	97.1
HH	Rear parcel box width	15.5	39.4
JJ	Steering wheel to seat cushion	8.6	21.9
KK	Steering wheel to seat squab	22.8	57.8
LL	Steering wheel reach adjustment	2.8	5.7
MM	Steering wheel diameter	15.0	38.1
NN	Maximum boot width	39.0	99.1
OO	Maximum boot length	41.0	104.1
PP	Maximum boot depth	10.3	25.0
QQ	Cubic capacity of boot	4.75 cu.ft.	0.133 cu.m.
RR	Maximum height boot open	56.1	142.7
SS	Maximum height bonnet open	58.3	148.0

All measurements are for an unladen car with seats in mid position total travel 5.75 ins. (14.61 cms.) with a 1 in. (2.5 cm.) rise.
N.B.: WEIGHT CONDITIONS:– Unladen – car with petrol on the road
Laden – car with petrol on the road with four persons and luggage.

THE 12-CYLINDER ANIMAL: JAGUAR V-12.

From its beginning several decades ago, Jaguar has always been Jaguar.

By that we mean that Jaguar has set its own benchmarks of what a car should be and has never deviated from its course. By following a course of personal conviction and conscience, its automobiles have achieved a high standard of individualism and spirit that in itself has become a standard for others.

Start with 1936, for that was the year of the S.S. Jaguar 100, a two-seater powered by the company's first effort at designing its own engine. Its success can be measured by the fact that it had the best individual performance overall in the famous International Alpine Trial competition of that year. Part of the reason was its road and cornering stability, an attribute that stemmed from its low center of gravity and wide tracking (features loudly proclaimed by today's car makers).

Then came the Jaguar that practically overnight rendered obsolete all that came before it in terms of sports car design and performance. The year, 1948. The car: the XK 120 which combined luxury comfort with magnificent performance. It was also the first quantity-produced car to be fitted with a twin-overhead camshaft engine. At the same time, its striking aerodynamic design was hailed for its purity of line. In the words of one observer, instead of following any school of design of the time, Jaguar's XK 120 created one.

Three years later, in 1951, Jaguar developed the lightweight XK-engined C-type that won the Le Mans 24-hour race the first time out. This was but the initial thrust of a spectacular invasion of Le Mans. The triumph was repeated again in 1953. Then the D-type, making its appearance in 1954, won the competition in 1955, 1956, and 1957. An enviable record, for those uncompromising auto-makers from Coventry.

In 1961 to match their pace-setting engineering with trend-setting design, Jaguar introduced the XKE. It set a styling standard which is still unequalled.

Now Jaguar has the long awaited V-12 that will do the same for engine standards. The excitement stems not just from a numbers perspective (although there is no disputing that 12 cylinders are impressive), but from the effortlessness and uncanny smoothness with which its power is produced.

The reason for this lies in the V-12's configuration: it is inherently balanced. Simply put, this means that there is a symmetry of forces within the engine's block.

Result: There are no "out of balance" factors from either a primary or a secondary source. Hence, smoothness of performance, not power for power's sake is the reason-for-being behind the V-12.

The Jaguar V-12 engine. The objective of Jaguar, in its engineering of the V-12 engine, was smoothness of engine performance. Not brute power □ Because of its inherent balance, the engine idles in near silence with virtually no vibration. It powers the Jaguar to 60 m.p.h. in 6.8 seconds with such sinuous grace that one hardly experiences a sensation of motion. And even at full 6500 rpm there is an eerie absence of engine noise □ Of significance is its power to displacement ratio. Jaguar's V-12 displaces only 326 cubic inches and yet develops 314 horsepower □ Of additional significance is its power-to-engine weight ratio. The total engine weight: an unexpected 680 pounds. Reason: the Jaguar V-12 engine is almost all aluminum □ The V-12's flat head design (with a single camshaft per bank as a natural corollary) was chosen only after tests with various designs plus previous experience gained with Coventry Climax racing engines. The V-12's flat head design produces excellent torque throughout the lower and middle speed ranges. This is especially useful in today's city-to-thruway kind of driving □ The bore/stroke measurements are also rather unusual—a 3½-inch bore and a 2¾-inch stroke. This means the cylinder is unusually wide and the piston stroke unusually short. The advantage: it provides lower piston speed for longer engine life □ Another revolutionary development: a transistorized ignition system. This system, race-proven in Formula 1 cars, employs a new electronic distributor that eliminates all contact points. With no contact points to wear or foul, a major cause of engine tune-ups is eliminated. (Incidentally, an out-of-tune engine is a major cause of engine pollution.) □ Every single V-12 engine—not just an occasional one—is thoroughly and exhaustively tested. Besides individual testing of components, each engine with its clutch and gearbox is bench-tested as a unit—not once but several times. (Final engine approval, of course, is reserved until 2 different road tests by 2 different crews.) □ This then is Jaguar's latest contribution to automotive history: the new V-12. In our opinion, it is the finest production engine in any automobile, regardless of size, regardless of price.

The Jaguar 2 + 2.

The 2 + 2, like all Jaguars, takes 8 full weeks to build. It is, of course, a sports car. An enclosed sports car with a host of amenities for touring in the grand style.

The suspension system.

All four wheels are fully independently suspended. A bump on one does not lift another. This isn't mere creature comfort—although it is comfortable—it is creature safety. Moreover, new front-end "anti-dive" geometry, plus torsion bars, has been introduced into the suspension system to make the 2 + 2 sure-footed. And for even surer footing, the track has been appreciably widened.

The steering.

When you turn the wheel, you turn the wheels. No more. No less. The steering is power-assisted rack-and-pinion with 3.5 turns lock-to-lock. And the steering column is adjustable. For extra maneuverability, the turning circle has been reduced from 41 to 36 feet.

The amenities.

The reclining bucket seats are upholstered in top-quality leather of matching color and grain. They fold forward to facilitate entrance and exit to the back seat.

The back seat, in turn, pivots forward to add extra room to the already generous luggage space. A wide-swinging rear door, with an interior release, provides quick and easy access to the luggage compartment.

A most important amenity: a new flow-through ventilation system with an air extractor louver situated on the car's rear panel.

The Jaguar 2 + 2. The ultimate cat. With a permanent roof.

The Jaguar Convertible.
Several changes have been made in the Convertible enhancing its design. The bumper-brakelight assembly, for example, has been restyled so the lights are now an integral part of the wrap-around bumper. And underneath the bumper is an impressive array of tail-pipes.

The Convertible now measures 15 feet 4 inches in overall length. This adds several extra inches of leg room and trunk room. In addition, doors have been widened to provide for easy entrance and exit.

The newly designed all-weather top can be quickly and easily raised or lowered. It's so snug-fitting you're comfortable even in the most severe weather conditions.

The Jaguar Convertible. The ultimate cat. With a folding top.

The ultimate cat: outside. The ultimate cat has had exterior changes. The fenders are slightly flared. This animal not only claws the road, it also looks like it does. And there's a new unity in the design of the headlamps, parking lights, and turn signals, accentuated by the sweep of the wrap-around bumper. As indicated by the 2 + 2 (below), this animal — even at rest — seems ready to spring.

The grille gleams through an oval of chrome. And at its center, the distinguished symbol of Jaguar. Beneath the grille, the new air scoop for more efficient engine ventilation. (Incidentally, eight coats of paint are applied to the body — the last one after the car has been road-tested.)

This is the ultimate cat. Lithe. Sleek. Swift. Adapted to any motoring environment. With independent 4-wheel suspension to give this animal the footing it needs, regardless of the surface it's running on. With power-assisted rack-and-pinion steering. And a new power-assisted braking system with 10-inch discs in back and new 11-inch ventilated discs in front. When you want this cat to stop in its tracks, it stops.

126

The ultimate cat: inside.
The front bucket seats recline
individually and fold forward to facilitate
passage to and from the back seat in the
2 + 2 model. Additionally, the back of
the rear seat pivots forward to provide
the abundant luggage space illustrated
on the opposite page. Standard on all
models: a retractable, inertia-reel
seat-belt system.

Some of the cat's equipment.
Included in the price of every
Jaguar is a center console-
mounted synchromesh 4-speed
stick shift. The instrument panel,
including the electric tachometer,
is designed for accessibility
visually and manually. As a safety
feature, all metal parts, such as
instrument surrounds and heater
controls, are finished with a
non-reflective surface. The
diameter of the adjustable steering
wheel has been reduced to 15
inches. The steering wheel itself
has satin-finished aluminum alloy
spokes and a rim covered in
hand-stitched leather.

The Jaguar interior (below) is a suitable setting indeed for the owner of such an extraordinary sports car. Complete instrumentation, including tachometer (second dial from left). A transistorized clock, flanked by gauges, is highlighted by a map light. Notice the neat row of rocker switches below the gauges. They control the auxiliary systems. The four-speed manual transmission is standard. An automatic is optional.

Classic good looks are apparent everywhere—from the sculptured seats with head-restraints to the arrangement of the front and side lighting. The side mounted mirror is adjustable from inside. And the classic Jaguar convertible (below) can be fitted with an optional removable hardtop. The chrome-plated wire wheels and whitewall tires are also optional.

There are two Jaguar E-type V-12 models.
The 2+2 is in the background and the convertible
roadster is in the foreground.

Summary of standard features:

Jaguar V-12, aluminum-alloy engine.

Independent suspension, front and rear with
"anti-dive" control.

Power-assisted four-wheel disc brakes, ventilated in front.

Power-assisted rack and pinion steering.

Four-speed manual transmission (an automatic
is optional).

Seats faced with genuine English leather.

Leather wrapped steering wheel.

Complete sports car instrumentation.

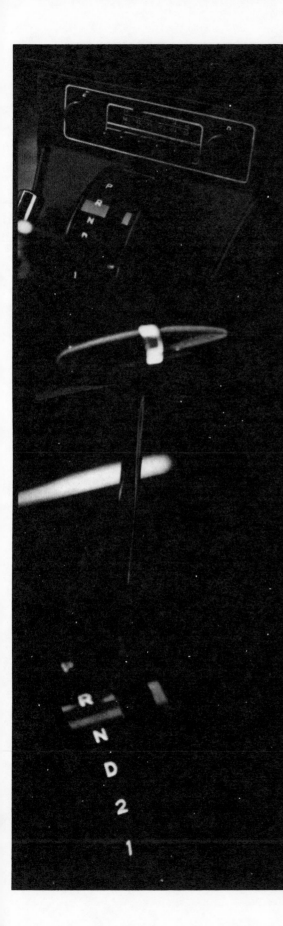

Optional equipment.

The list of options for the Jaguar E-type V-12 is rather limited. This is simply because all the essentials and many of the amenities are included in the basic price.

Among the Jaguar's optional equipment you may wish to consider:

Automatic transmission.

Factory-installed air conditioning.

Solid-state AM/FM multiplex radio.

Chrome wire wheels or chrome turbo-disc wheels.

Radial-ply whitewall tires.

Electrically heated demisting rear window (on the 2 + 2).

Tinted glass.

Custom-fitted removable hardtop (on the convertible).

Capture a Jaguar.

The Jaguar E-type is a glorious thing to have and to hold.

No ordinary motor car this. But a creature of fire and spirit, whose every movement is pure poetry.

For all who have eyes to see, the Jaguar E-type is a classic piece of sculpture and was cited for excellence of design by the Museum of Modern Art.

But for those with both eyes and insight, the classic Jaguar styling is only the outward sign of an extraordinary sophistication beneath the surface.

The E-type's steel monocoque body is of the type used in advanced racing machinery.

The power-assisted four-wheel disc brakes (pioneered by Jaguar at Le Mans) are ventilated in front and mounted inboard in the rear.

The fully independent suspension system matched to Dunlop SP 70 radials, provides a cat-like combination of grace and sure-footedness.

Power-assisted rack and pinion steering adds to the precision of handling and tracking.

And the silken smooth Jaguar V-12 aluminum alloy engine brings it all to life. It has only 326 cubic inches of capacity, yet it performs with a degree of smoothness and quietness that's more like a turbine than an internal combustion engine.

Of course, in the cockpit, you'll find a complete array of instrumentation and controls, plus a level of excellence in workmanship and materials that is the hallmark of Jaguar.

So if you yearn for a sports car that has been a classic from the first, set your sights on a Jaguar E-type—the ultimate cat.

You'll find one lurking at your Jaguar dealer. For his name call (800) 447-4700. In Illinois, call (800) 322-4400. Calls are toll free.

BRITISH LEYLAND MOTORS INC., LEONIA, N.J. 07605

Jaguar V-12: The ultimate cat

The reason: Jaguar's new aluminum 12-cylinder engine. Quite possibly, the most exciting automotive development in a decade.

The inherently balanced nature of the V-12 configuration produces an almost uncanny smoothness. There is an absence of vibration even at low speeds. And yet the V-12 can hit 70 m.p.h. with such sinuous grace that one hardly experiences the sensation of motion.

But what's so important is not the absolute power it is capable of producing but the delivery of that power through an exceptionally wide range. Result: the ultimate cat performs as well in congested city traffic as on a wide-open thruway.

Some specifics:

(1) The engine displaces only 326 cubic inches and yet develops 314 horsepower for an efficient displacement-to-power ratio.

(2) In the V-12's flathead design, the cylinders have a large bore and the pistons a short stroke for higher potential power and longer engine life.

(3) The new transistorized ignition system employs an electronic distributor with no contact points to wear or foul. Significance: A major cause of engine tuneups is eliminated.

Additional virtues: The fully independent suspension with "anti-dive" geometry to counter front-end dipping. Rack-and-pinion steering, power-assisted with 3.5 turns lock to lock. Four-wheel disc brakes, also power-assisted and self-adjusting.

Jaguar 2+2 with the revolutionary V-12 engine—the ultimate cat. See it at your Jaguar dealer. And, for a sight you'll never forget, look under the hood.

For the name of your nearest Jaguar dealer, dial (800) 631-1971 except in New Jersey where the number is (800) 962-2803. Calls are toll-free.

BRITISH LEYLAND MOTORS INC., LEONIA, N. J. 07605

Jaguar V-12